What others are s̶ ̶ ̶ ̶ ̶ ̶ ̶ ̶ ̶ ̶ ̶

Stand

"Behind the cover of 'Stand' lie pages of understanding and truth for the challenges teens face. Shannon offers practical guidance for navigating through the "tough years" while sharing stories and experiences that remind readers they are not alone. As my mentor, the words of warmth, understanding, support, and guidance she shares in this book were some of the very words that moved me from drowning in my "tough years" to overcoming them. She disproves that "adults don't understand," while also offering hope and wisdom."

> **–Sarah Benefiel,** *M.A. Clinical Mental Health Counseling*

"Shannon Perry dives deep into the world of a teenage girl. 'Stand' is a unique book, written with real teen girls with real teen struggles. Without sounding "preachy," Shannon gives practical, Biblical advice to navigate through the rough waters of teen life. "Stand" shows teen girls how to not just survive, but to thrive!"

> **–Kennis Russell,** *Associate Pastor/Youth Director at Christ Family Church*

"Combining informative information with scriptural principles, Shannon Perry offers practical, yet timeless advice..."

> **– Josh McDowell,** *Popular speaker, Josh McDowell Ministry/A division of Campus Crusade for Christ International*

"Shannon loves Jesus, loves people and is passionate about helping young people. In the pages of 'Stand,' she gives attention to truth in a world that often screams lies. My church hosted an "In Her Shoes" event and moms and teens alike were challenged, inspired and encouraged!"
— **Rhonda Mohr,** *Family Life Minister*

Stand

Stand

Staying Balanced with Answers for Real Teen Life

SHANNON PERRY

For resources and speaking information:
www.ShannonPerry.com, or write to Chae Music,
P.O. Box 2887, Cypress, TX 77410-2887

Dedicated to

"B.P.," affectionately known as "Baby Perry." I pray that all I have shared in this book will be helpful to you when you are a teenager one day. Even though we haven't met yet, I already love you.

Stand:

a. An attitude toward a particular issue; a position taken in an argument

b. Have or maintain an upright position, supported by one's feet

c. Withstand an experience or test without being damaged

Acknowledgements

Study Group Girls– Your input into this project is priceless and your love for God and His direction is amazing. Your willingness to share the "hard stuff" that teens experience helped to shape this book. Thank you for your faithfulness each week and for "digging deep" to find the answers that work. We did it!

Back row, left to right:
Allison, Lauren, Camryn, Amanda, Mariah, Mrs. Perry
Front row, left to right:
Alicia, Brianna, Avery, Phaedra, Macy, Brynne

Sharon Taylor– You knew everything about me as a teenager, and loved me anyway. Thank you for being my teacher, mentor and friend. You modeled God's amazing love to me and forty years later, your influence continues. I love you.

Sarah, Gina, Mom and Laurie– Thank you for your tireless efforts to make every detail of this book its best. I couldn't ask for a better editing team. I love and appreciate each of you so very much.

Chloe, Avery and Sophia– Thank you for taking a "stand" on the cover of this book. You are beautiful inside and out!

Di Ann Mills– Thank you for your continual, yet gentle nudge to write yet another book and for the editing help as I began. You may be small, but you are quite big in my world!

Christy– Thank you for all the Dr. Pepper, words of encouragement and laughs as I worked each day. I pray that all who read this book are blessed with the kind of friend that you have been to me.

To all those who gave to the "In Her Shoes" tour so that this book became a necessity, thank you. I am forever grateful to you for the lives we will be allowed to touch because of your generosity.

To THE Author and Finisher of my Faith, Jesus Christ– "Standing" with you through this life has been my greatest joy.

Table of Contents

Chapters

Appendices

SHANNON PERRY

"In Her Shoes"

Written for the Mother/Teen Daughter Conference "In Her Shoes"

© 2015 Peggy Dykes and Shannon Perry

I wonder what it feels like to be her
Pages in the magazine are so far from her world
Broken by the promises a friend would never keep
She tries to smile but cries herself to sleep
Dreaming of the day he will come her way
There's one thing she needs to hear me say

Chorus:
I'll take a walk in your shoes
Praying that truth
Will build the bridge between me and you
With every step we take love will be the way I choose
To take a walk in your shoes.

I wonder what it feels like to be her
Everything about me is her greatest concern
Will I learn the lessons that she's tried so hard to teach
Or turn my head to stay out of her reach
When our worlds collide she stays by my side
Maybe now it's time for me to choose

Chorus

One day we will see
More than you and me
Walking down the road that we will choose

Chorus

SHANNON PERRY

Prologue

As a teenager, I didn't always see eye-to-eye with my parents because I felt like they didn't *get* me. I tried to do the right things, but I often blew it. Don't get me wrong, I wasn't a bad kid. I went to church and was very involved at school, but somehow I needed more. I needed answers that were easy to understand and that would work so that I could figure out how to *do* the teenage life.

A lot of days, it seemed like everyone else had it together, and I was one big mess. Some days I felt like I didn't fit in, like no one understood me and that I was hopelessly unattractive to the cute boys in school. Everyone else told me I was beautiful, but I was frustrated by my feelings that seemed to change all the time. Sometimes, I didn't even understand myself!

For those reasons and more, I wrote "Stand." My goal is to offer you practical answers to situations you may face as a teen. I have also included truths from the Bible, but hopefully I have done it in a way that you will not feel like I am "preaching" to you. A wonderful group of teen girls helped me write this study and they told me there are two things teens don't like: "Being talked down to" and "Someone 'preaching' to" them. While the Bible is the best guidebook for the decisions we will make in life, I kept my study group's advice in mind while writing.

This book is written out of love and compassion for you, knowing the teen life can have its challenges. If you are reading this book alone or studying it with a group, my prayer is that it will be a useful tool to help you find answers in every area you may be facing.

CHAPTER ONE

Boys

"Ladies you deserve to be his first place girl, not his just in case girl."

—*Unknown*

Boys. Just the word can cause emotions to explode inside of us. Some days, they're wonderful. Other days, guys act weird and we hardly know them by how quickly they change.

Having a healthy relationship with a guy is possible, but how do we do it?

One of the first things we must embrace is this simple truth: guys and girls are different. Girls tell guys they need space when they often want him to show he cares. A guy takes her request for space literally, and leaves her alone. Guys are visually stimulated while girls are emotionally stimulated. We feel good when someone tells us we're beautiful. Guys feel good when they see someone beautiful. While both are "normal," the trouble comes when we don't keep our feelings in check. Guys "rate" girls by their backside and chest instead of their heart and personality, so girls work tirelessly to change their body shape to gain a good "rating." Our study group knows of one girl who even went as far as putting water balloons in her bra so her chest would look bigger! She thought it was a great idea - until they popped during lunchtime!

So, how can we know if we're getting involved with the right guy? One thing we should always do is take time to get to know him. Watch his actions in all areas. Is he clingy or excessively complimentary? Does he send one-word replies to texts or apologize constantly? These behaviors can be annoying and get worse the longer we date. Can you trust his character? After all, many guys claim to be Christians, but what if their actions are far from Christ-like?

When a guy is controlling, checks your phone, manipulative or a cheater, he is not Christ-like and he is not for you. We are reminded in 2 Corinthians 6:14 that we are not to be "yoked together" with unbelievers. That includes our dating life. In biblical times, a yoke was used to keep oxen together when they would plow the fields. If one ox was bigger than the other, the bigger one would dominate and the rows would be crooked. So, what does an ox have to do with your dating relationship? When you're "yoked" with a dating partner who doesn't have the same morals and beliefs that you do, you may be dominated and the rows of your life can become very crooked.

When Debby was 16, she started dating Scott, the quarterback of the football team. He was "hot" and their relationship was the talk of the school. They were *perfect* together, and Debby thought so too... until she found out that Scott smoked pot. Debby knew it was wrong, but she reasoned that Scott could have been doing worse things, so she went along with it. One night while they were out on a date, Scott got pulled over. When the cops opened the door, a bag of weed fell out of the car. Immediately, Scott pointed to Debby. Debby desperately tried to tell the police it wasn't hers, but she was guilty by association. They were both cuffed, and taken to juvenile detention for questioning. Debby quickly learned that being "yoked" with someone can be a really bad deal when morals are different.

Cute guys don't always have cute character. Proverbs 27:19 says, "As water reflects the face, so one's life reflects the heart." We know a person's heart by the way they live. You may be dating a cute guy, but does he treat you one way in private and another way in public? Does he kiss you in private then act like he doesn't know you in public? Does he make you feel like you're not good enough or that he is even ashamed of you? If so, there's nothing cute about him or the way he treats you.

When a guy truly cares about you, he will treat you with the same respect and adoration in public that he does in private. If he tells you that you are beautiful in private, he will do so in public, even at the cost of getting made fun of by friends. He is not afraid to let others know that he is with you. If he does not treat you the same publicly as he does privately, a conversation needs to take place about your feelings. If he disregards those feelings or continues to ignore you in public, the relationship should end. You are worth far more than being someone's secret girlfriend.

One of the greatest dangers girls face when they begin going out with a guy is getting sucked into the "boy vortex." You know how that goes. You've either seen it happen to one of your friends, or you've done it yourself. You begin going out with a guy, and all of a sudden, your brain becomes incapacitated. All you think about is *him*. You go to sleep thinking about *him*. You wake up talking to a friend about *him*. As a matter of fact, he's ALL you ever talk about! You start dressing in clothes you think *he'll* like, you smile the way you think *he* would like and you walk the way you think *he* would like. Before you know it, you don't even know what YOU like anymore because your world has become all about what *he* likes. No more Friday nights out with friends to watch sappy chick flicks. Friday night is now reserved exclusively for him. Actually, EVERY night is reserved for him.

When our world revolves solely around a guy, we lose perspective, we often lose friends and we lose our identity. If you have built your world around your guy, get your brain and perspective back - and do it quickly! Tell him you would like to spend some time with friends on the weekend. Wear clothes YOU feel good in and do things YOU enjoy. If you question whether or not you are in the "boy vortex," ask your friends. They will quickly tell you if you are building your world around your guy.

We must also remember that we do not have the power to change anyone. Too many times, we miss the glaring and unappealing truths about a guy because we keep hoping he will change. We also play the "if only" game. "If only" he were more sensitive and would talk about his feelings. "If only" he were smarter so we could study together.

Sometimes we want change but we don't trust what we're feeling. For example, your guy gets mad, yanks your keys out of your hands, and throws them across the parking lot. You stand stunned, wondering what just happened. He apologizes, says he'll never do it again and gives you roses. You feel ashamed that you ever thought badly of him... until he does it the next time. He promises he'll change, buys you more roses, and you forgive him again. While he may or may not change, you must ask yourself two very important questions: Do I have the power to change him, and why would I want to put up with someone that may explode like this again? While you may not know the answer to the second question, I can give you the answer to the first one: NO! We do not have the power to change anyone. We never have, and we never will. If a guy chooses to change, allow him to do that away

If a guy chooses to change, allow him to do that away from you and then test his character again.

from you and then test his character again. Allow some time so that he and God can work on his life while you continue on with your life. We will have the healthiest relationships when we allow our world to revolve around what God wants for our life, and not around a guy. God knows how to find the "good guys."

So, what do guys worth dating look for in a girl? It might surprise you. While guys I spoke to quickly admitted to liking a girl who looks good, they also said they would not want a long-term relationship with a girl who dresses inappropriately. They admitted they do initially look when a girl is dressed immodestly, but they also wonder, "Why does that girl think she has to dress like that? What kind of insecurity is she hiding?" If your guy doesn't think like this, you may want to reconsider. After all, we want a guy who appreciates what's in the heart under the dress, right?

The guys I spoke with also admitted to wanting a long-term relationship with girls who are confident and fun. Girls who are clingy, needy, or dependent, put pressure on them and they typically shy away from those girls, no matter how good they look. If you're hanging on the car door yelling, "I love you!" when a boy tries to leave your driveway, be assured he won't be around for long. While that might look romantic in a movie, guys think it's weird. Stalking a guy or smothering him with "love" will quickly drive him to someone else.

Sometimes, guys do things that make us ask, "Why?" It's so hard to understand why they are so indecisive or why they think saying, "I'm sorry," fixes everything. Most guys want to succeed at relationships as much as girls do, but they don't always know how to do it. As girls, we think they should do one thing, while as guys, they think something totally different. Remember those differences? Here's where the frustration comes into play. When a guy is indecisive, it's usually because he is unsure of himself. He wants to make the right decision, but because he doesn't know what the right decision is, he bounces back and forth between answers. Sometimes it's because he is noncommittal. You will know after watching how he treats you over time.

When a guy says he's sorry, believe him until he proves otherwise. Our part is to forgive him, but nowhere does the Bible say that forgiveness means we have to have a relationship with that person. If he hurts you and you can't trust him not to do it again, end the relationship. Just keep forgiveness in your heart so his actions don't have a long-term effect on you.

Once you consider entering a relationship with a guy, it's important to continually test his heart and make sure his motives are pure. Testing his heart doesn't mean asking him if he likes your dress or that you go scrolling through his phone to see who his latest "woman crush" is. Testing his heart means watching his actions and believing his actions above his words.

"Actions speak louder than words" is a great cliché to always include in your dating life. When a guy is Christ-like, attentive, respectful, and trustworthy, we see what the Bible defines as love. Love is not just romantic. It's how we should be treated as well as how we should treat others. The Bible defines love in 1 Corinthians 13. I challenge you to read and study the attributes of love for all your relationships. Unfortunately, some girls settle for less because they believe they are only lovable when they are in a relationship, even if it is a bad one.

If you have ever been in a bad relationship, you know the stress and unbearable heartache it brings. If you have not had a bad relationship and want to know some signs to watch for so that you can avoid being in one, the following may be of help:

* He flirts with your friends and says, "It's no big deal."

* Your relationship is filled with drama.

* You're pressured to give yourself physically because he threatens to leave if you don't.

* You make suggestions or set boundaries that are not respected.

* He says, "Friends with physical benefits is okay."

* He treats you one way in public and another way in private.

If you find yourself in an unhealthy relationship, here are some things you may want to consider:

1. What are your deal breakers? What does a guy have to do/not do before you decide not to have a relationship with him?

2. What boundaries do you have in place for your relationship so that unhealthy behavior is avoided?

3. Are you willing to accept unacceptable behavior from a guy? Why or why not?

In our study group, deal breakers include drugs; abuse/illegal use of alcohol; verbal, sexual, emotional or physical abuse; cheating; dishonesty and not being a "real" Christian.

While we've talked about dating and boys, friendship with a guy can be equally important. Can you be "just friends" with a guy? Some say you can't, but our study group believes you can. Being clear about the relationship you want to have is key.

The "friend zone" can be a good place to be with a guy. It can also get complicated when one of you wants to be friends, but the other wants more. If you find yourself wanting only a friendship with a guy, be very clear with him. Don't "sugar coat" how you feel and state upfront that you are only interested in being friends. If he insists on being more, you may have to back away to clearly state your expectations. Don't be afraid to "friend zone" your guy friend because he might stop being your friend. He will stay if your friendship is strong. Don't back down for fear of hurting his feelings and telling him you only want to be friends. You will hurt him much more in the long run if you pretend to like him, and actually don't. What could be a good friendship will most certainly end in disaster if you pretend to have feelings that are not there.

> **When your friend's motives are pure, he can see things in other guys that you may not see and help protect you from making a mistake.**

Sometimes, the tables are turned. You begin a friendship with a guy only to find yourself attracted to him as the friendship progresses. Now what? If you find that he only wants to be friends, you must respect his decision and understand there are many more guys out there. God may be using your guy friend to help you learn about the boys you will date down the road. It's always good to have a guy friend to talk to about boys you like. When your friend's motives are pure, he can see things in other guys that you may not see, and help protect you from making a mistake. If you sense your friend's motives may not be pure and he asks more often than he should about your dating relationship with someone else, gently remind him that you are not discussing details with him. If he persists, tell him lovingly to mind his own business.

Girl friends are also great when discussing dating relationships, but we must remember that we are not able to resolve our friend's dating issues. Many times, it will only cause more damage if we try to point out the obvious to our girlfriend about her dating disaster. If she doesn't see it, you can't make her. We can advise friends using God's Word and past experience, but we must also know that we are not responsible for fixing another's dating dilemma.

Katy saw her friend Jill dating a guy that was not good for her. Collin liked Jill, but he liked her when it was convenient for him. He would call Jill one day, and then wait a week before calling again. When Jill confronted Collin asking why he didn't call more, he said he'd just been busy and assured her it was no big deal. It was a big deal to Jill, but she tried to blow it off because she really liked Collin. After three months of watching Jill's heart get yanked around, Katy confronted Jill. She lovingly told Jill that she was concerned about Collin's inconsistency. Katy had seen Collin playing basketball at his house in his spare time, and knew Collin could be calling Jill more if he really wanted to talk. When Katy reminded Jill that she was a "convenience" for Collin, Jill exploded. Instead of trusting Katy to have her best interest at heart, Jill got mad and accused Katy of being jealous because she had a boyfriend and Katy didn't. Katy left the relationship feeling hurt, and now they no longer speak.

Sometimes, friends must discover their dating disasters on their own. There are times, however, when it is appropriate to take action when you sense your friend is in danger. If you find that your girlfriend is sharing details of her dating life that involve abuse in any way, tell her you are concerned. Let her know that you are there to listen, and encourage her to talk with adults who can help. If she refuses to get help, go to an adult who can help her. The last thing any of us want is for our friends to be injured or mistreated. While they may ask us not to tell, the best thing we can do for them is to get an adult involved who can intervene before it is too late. Too many girls have disappeared or been grossly misused in a dating situation because someone was afraid to tell. Be safe, but inform their parents or another adult who can intervene. You should never try to step in and handle an abusive situation on your own. You are placing yourself in harm's way and will only endanger your friend further.

Although they can be complicated at times, relationships with guys can be very rewarding. They teach us about ourselves, and help us figure out what we want and don't want in a future date and mate. Our study group believes that there are some key reminders that every teen girl should consider when dating and some of those reminders are listed below. You may want to post these encouraging messages on your mirror or a place you see often as a daily reminder:

* Healthy boundaries include keeping your clothes on, sending and receiving text messages

your grandma could read, and not doing anything you have to hide.

It is okay to say, "NO!"

* You are good enough. If a guy makes you feel like you're not, he's not the one.

* It is okay to say, "NO!"

* Constant drama is like a baseball game. Three strikes and you're out.

* You CAN wait! Never let a guy manipulate you.

* Trust, communication, boundaries, honesty, and values must be before looks. Cute is good. Cute with integrity is great.

* Putting yourself and your standards first isn't selfish, it's essential.

* Whoever you date is a potential mate.

* Never change for a boy, but be all God created you to be. Psalm 139:13 is a great reminder.

Reflections:

> ➢ What are some ways that guys and girls act differently? How will you handle those differences?

> ➢ What does Psalm 139:14 mean to you personally when it says that you are "fearfully and wonderfully made?"

> ➢ Have you ever felt disregarded or not "good enough" when dating a guy? How did you handle it?

> ➢ 2 Corinthians 6:14 is often used with adults when they're getting married, but what does it mean to you to be "equally yoked" in your dating life?

> ➢ Have you ever liked a guy but secretly wanted to change something about him? What did you do and what was the result?

> ➢ What does it look like for you to let your world revolve around what God wants for your life instead of what a guy wants?

> ➢ What do you think a healthy dating relationship will look like for you?

CHAPTER TWO

Taking Out the Trash

"A woman is not written in braille. You don't have to touch her to know her."

—Unknown

What are your morals? Have you given it much thought? Are morals just something you have when it works well, or are they set in stone in your heart? God has given us some very specific guidelines regarding morals in His Word and if we follow them, we can have great success in our lives. In Psalm 119:9, David writes, "How can a young person stay pure? By obeying God's Word and following its rules." If we don't follow God's plan for us, the outcome can be disastrous.

I'm grateful I had my mom and dad to help guide my choices in high school. They knew how to help me draw strong boundaries when I really didn't WANT to draw those boundaries. I was a junior and the cutest boy in the school asked me to go to the beach with him and some friends. He could drive, but I was not allowed to travel more than an hour away from home. There were girls and guys going on this trip, but there were no

31

chaperones going. My mom and dad immediately told me I could not go. No chaperones, no Shannon. I was VERY upset. After all, the cutest boy in the school liked me! I cried and begged my parents to let me go, but the answer was always the same: "No." How do parents do it? How can they look you in the eye when you're crying and begging and be so matter of fact? I didn't understand then, and I thought my life was over. How would I ever face any of my friends again?

I called the cutest boy in the school and told him I couldn't go. I will never forget when he said, "Oh Shannon, it's okay. We can just hang out and do something near your house. I just invited you because I want to get to know you better." WHAT? The cutest boy in the school wants to get to know ME? I got off the phone and jumped up and down on my bed like a crazy person screaming, "He just wants to get to know me!" My parents thought I had lost it.

What happens when we meet a guy who really cares about us? He will respect our morals and want to spend time with us, even when he doesn't get his way. I am happy to say that I did date that guy for a while and he turned out to be a very good friend. He became a pro football player and when I run into him, he hugs me and is very kind to this day. We can never go wrong when we keep our morals. Others will respect us, and we will respect ourselves.

Guys with pure motives will also respect our parents and their wishes. When our parents say be home by eleven, he brings us home five minutes early.

Philippians 4:8 says, "Whatsoever things are PURE, lovely or of good report, think on these things." Purity, by definition, is anything free of contamination or pollution. It would be gross to walk around smelling trash all day. Who wants contamination or pollution in their life? To live a life of purity, we have to take out the trash.

The girls in our study group believe it is important to remain pure in our dating lives. To help us remain pure in times of temptation, we need to have some guidelines in place. When we think of

To live a life of purity, we have to take out the trash.

solutions to situations we might encounter ahead of time, we can be ready when we are tempted to compromise in the heat of the moment. For example, let's pretend you're on a date. The two of you are having a wonderful conversation as you're driving. Suddenly, your date pulls off on a side street and parks in a dark place. He turns off the car, looks at you, and smiles. Now what? If you think he's just there to listen to music, guess again. At this moment, it would be in your best interest, and his, to suggest that you keep driving and get into a lighted area as soon as possible. Oh, I know your hormones may be telling you to do something else. After all, this guy is "hot!" Let him know you really like him and that you want to do things that will make both of you comfortable the next time you see each other. Is this easy? Hardly! It is worth it however, because you will have a relationship of respect and trust and those relationships usually last a lot longer than those that blow up like a firecracker in the heat of passion. Once the firecracker blows up, you can never light it again.

Having a Christian mentor, parent or adult in our life that can hold us accountable is a great first step if we want to keep our dating life pure. It is far too easy to contaminate our lives with trash if we don't have an adult we trust to remind us about the importance of respecting ourselves and remaining pure. We need to choose mentors we can trust to talk with about ANYTHING in our dating life. ANYTHING? Yes, *anything*. If we can't be transparent with them, they're not the right mentor. Our mentor should listen without reacting, guide us in our struggles, and lead us closer to purity by doing things God's way. A once-a-week meeting with your mentor is a great plan when you begin to date.

Recently one of my "mentees" came to me in tears about her dating life. Her boyfriend was trying to convince her that oral sex was not really sex and that it was okay as long as they didn't have actual sex. He told her he loved her and that he would never ask her to do anything that she was not comfortable doing. She was very uncomfortable with this idea and said she knew it was wrong. I listened and realized that her struggle was more than the issue at hand. It was about her boyfriend's selfishness. Not only was he asking her to do something she knew was wrong, he was presenting it in a way so she would feel guilty if she didn't do what he wanted her to do. After I listened, we looked up some scripture to see what God's Word says about any kind of sexual act before marriage. Guess what? There was plenty there to remind her that ANY kind of sex outside of marriage is wrong no matter how much her boyfriend tried to convince her otherwise. Hebrews 13:4 says, "Let the marriage bed be undefiled." That means no one should be a sexual partner to us until we are married. There are additional scriptures about purity in the back of this book, and I would strongly encourage you to read them. She found the courage to tell him, "No" and knew immediately she'd made the right decision when he got angry and broke up with her for not having sex with him.

Why is it so important that we keep our morals? After all, from every movie, video, television show and text, it seems like "everybody's doing it." Our study group would like to assure you EVERYONE IS NOT DOING IT. The girls in our study group have made a commitment to save themselves for their husbands. Why? Because they don't want to carry trash into their marriage bed. Once we are sexual in any way with a guy, we carry it with us FOREVER! Forever is a LONG time.

Staying pure with a guy we really like can be extremely challenging. After all, we're very attracted to him or we wouldn't be with him. When hormones rage and the heat of the moment is hotter than the sun, saying "No" is difficult! Guys know how to use lines that will make us want to believe him desperately. If you hear things like, "Oh baby, you know I love you, I just want to be close to you" it can be difficult to say "No." After all, that's hot! Other lines may be, "I will love you forever, don't worry, I'm not going anywhere," or "You're the only girl I have ever felt this way about." When a guy feeds you those lines, he doesn't love you, he wants to control you to get his way!

We all know that men like to hunt. They like the thrill of the hunt. But what happens once a guy catches what he is hunting? HE KILLS IT! It works the same way in relationships. Once a guy gets what he wants sexually in a relationship, he is often on to the next girl. It may not be right away, but most guys move on to higher hunting grounds. That's why you must always remain "the hunted." You must be the one that is worthy of the chase. Not the one who offers to trash up their lives and the life of the guy you're dating by compromising your morals. Impurity doesn't just affect you; it affects your date and your future spouse as well.

> **You must be the one that is worthy of the chase.**

The reason God commands us to wait until we're married to be physically intimate with a guy is because He is protecting us. He is not trying to withhold something from us. He knows that once we become physically intimate with a guy, there is a tie to him,

FOREVER. Just ask a girl who has given herself physically to a guy and then broken up with him. Most of them will tell you she regrets it. He moves on to another girl, is physically intimate with that girl, and now you're just a number. That is NOT what God designed sex to be. Sex comes with a lifetime commitment so that you're not just a number, you are THE number. Once you have given yourself away physically for the first time, there will NEVER be another first time. Now, if you have already experimented with sex, don't shut the book. There is great hope for you to begin again. We will discuss how to do that later in this chapter.

In case you're still tempted to experiment with sex outside of marriage, knowing that approximately 750,000 teenagers get pregnant every year may help you reconsider ("Teen Pregnancy Facts"). If you fantasize about quitting EVERYTHING in your life to take care of someone else for the next 18 years, you are definitely in the minority. I have never spoken to an unmarried teen who said, "I'm so glad I got pregnant." Their friends eventually went off to college and they were left alone. Contrary to what "Hollywood" promotes, most guys do NOT stay with or marry the teen mother of their child.

Another step we need to take in order to keep our dating life pure is dating for the right reasons. Too many girls feel they are not complete unless they have a boyfriend. We feel like something is wrong with us when it seems everyone else has a boyfriend, but we don't. This is a lie that gets us into trouble and bad relationships. Have you stopped to ask God, "Do you want me to have a boyfriend right now?" Maybe you should consider that there's absolutely nothing wrong with you for not having a boyfriend, but God is waiting to put the most awesome person into your path at just the right time.

> God loves you and you will never find a love greater than His.

Too many times we get into bad relationships because we feel we have to be loved by a guy. At the risk of sounding cliché, I'm going to say it… God loves you and you will never find a love greater than His. If you ever feel unlovable, you can trust Him to put the right guy into your path when He knows you are ready for a relationship. He does this, not because He thinks you have to have it, but because He cares about what you care about. I'll jump out on a limb and say He probably won't do it when you want Him to, but it will happen when it's *supposed* to happen. Don't push it and wind up in a relationship you regret.

One girl I know got into a very bad relationship when she felt pressured to date. Her friends accused her of being "gay" because she never went on a date, so to prove them wrong, she went out with a guy she met on the internet. When she met him, he was not sixteen as he claimed when they were talking online. He was twenty eight! To be courteous, she stayed at the restaurant where they met and had dinner with him. Before the night was over, he tried to get her to go back to his house. She refused, and a short time later, found out he was connected with a dangerous human trafficking ring.

Ladies, you are living in a culture where purity is not just about waiting until marriage to have sex, it's about saving your very life! There are approximately 20 to 30 million slaves of human trafficking in the world today and the average age of a slave is 12-14 years old ("11 Facts about Human Trafficking"). These are horrible statistics and you do not want to end up as one. No one is worth risking your life! If you have not spent time around someone and only know them online, NEVER volunteer to meet them somewhere. It is far too easy for others to pretend they are someone they're not. Making purity a part of our lives includes making wise decisions and remaining safe.

Technology has done a lot to make staying pure more difficult. Take "sexting" for example. People have the ability to send sexually graphic images or messages by texting, and while that is not physically having sex, it is another form of sex on a cheap and meaningless level. Sexual messages sent through any form of technology are cheap and give us a false sense of intimacy. We allow ourselves to be used as a pawn, and the true intimacy that is desired is nowhere in sight. Guys who use technology as a "fantasy tool" are cowards, and show a lack of respect for you. Don't fall for it.

Not only is sexting disrespectful, it is punishable by crime in many states. When sexually explicit images, videos or messages are received or sent on your phone, they can be traced. Legally, you or your parents can be fined up to $1,000, ordered to mandatory counseling, and have your driving privileges restricted. Is it worth it? Hardly.

Technology also gives someone you're dating the opportunity to share your private life with anyone. Once a picture, video or message has been shared, they may choose to hit the "send button" at any time and launch your private life into the universe for all to see. Since this information is saved on a server for many years, it can affect your school status, college and job applications. It may even affect your future marriage if used as a weapon against you. Be very particular about what you publish on your phone or computer. It doesn't go away.

If you find that you shared something you regret and now others are sharing it online, it's never too late to get help. You can report photos and videos to the websites they are on or seek help from an adult you trust. Most websites do their best to remove embarrassing or hurtful videos and pictures once they are reported.

Purity is also a tried and proven method for avoiding disease. Abstinence, or avoiding sex of *any* kind, is a guarantee against sexually transmitted diseases. Sexually Transmitted Infections (STI's) are easily contracted when sex of any kind occurs. STI's are spread through oral, vaginal or anal sex and through genital touching. Contrary to popular belief, it is possible to contract an STI without having intercourse. You can't tell if a person is infected because many STI's have no symptoms. Even when there are no symptoms, an STI can be passed from one person to another. Many STI's are currently incurable and will be with you for the rest of your life. What's worse, they will be something you share with your future spouse. Not the ideal way to start off your honeymoon, is it? Why does God tell us to "avoid the hint of sexual immorality" in Ephesians 5:3? Because He knows the life-long damage it can do when we "play" with sexual temptation. There is NO "safe" sex outside of marriage.

"But what if I just play around and don't go too far?" Consider the following: Compromising your morals and your values IS going too far. This is why you must have them in place before you date. If a guy touches you in a way that makes you want to do more than watch TV, it's too far. You must also consider this question: Will I be able to look back ten years from now and be proud of the way I acted? The biggest challenge for girls is to keep a guard over their heart. The minute you believe something even hints at sexual impurity, throw your guard up and run. You will be glad in the long run. "But it feels so natural," you might say. However, feelings,

> Compromising your morals and your values IS going too far.

when used over logic, can take us down roads we don't want to travel. A good rule of thumb is this: If you have to ask, "Is this too far?" it probably is.

So what if we've already messed up? I've got good news! Jesus Christ gave His life so that we can be healed from past mistakes. He can forgive you and give you a new start TODAY when you ask Him for one. This is what His grace is all about. No, you can't get back what's been lost, but you can begin doing things His way right now. We've all messed up, and we all need forgiveness. Don't allow shame to tell you it's too late to start over. THAT IS A LIE. God wants to walk with you into every situation in your life. I John 1:9 says, "If we confess our sins, He is faithful and just to forgive us and PURIFY us." He can restore the purity you have lost and make you a new creation in Him (2 Corinthians 5:17). He loves you and has great plans just for you when you turn away from making your own decisions and allow Him to help you make the right ones.

Reflections:

- ➤ What are three advantages of remaining pure?

- ➤ What does the definition of purity mean to you?

- ➤ What are your morals? How will you keep those morals in place when you are in a tempting situation?

- ➤ Are you willing to have a mentor who will hold you accountable about your dating life? If so, who could you consider asking?

- ➤ What are your thoughts about having any level of sex outside of marriage?

- ➤ What do you base your beliefs on?

- ➤ How do you feel when you don't have a boyfriend and others do?

- ➤ What do you know about human trafficking? How can you avoid becoming a victim?

- ➤ Why is it important to avoid the "technology trap?"

- ➤ What do you find hardest about saying "No" when a guy you like tries to pursue you in ways that feel good but you know are wrong?

- ➤ If you or someone you know has already been sexually impure, how can they start over today?

SHANNON PERRY

CHAPTER THREE

friendship

"A good friend knows all your stories. A best friend helped you write them."

—Unknown

The best mirror that we can have in our lives is a great friend. They help us see clearly when our world is foggy, make us laugh, let us cry, keep our secrets, wipe our tears, stand up for us, hold us accountable, and love us through it all. Friends are one of the few things in life that we get to choose, and we need to choose wisely. Proverbs 17:17 says, "A friend loves at all times." Friendship is an "equal opportunity" relationship, and both friends must take responsibility for the friendship to work.

So what does a good friend look like? Our study group believes there are some key characteristics that must be present in order to have a healthy friendship. One of those is open communication.

Communication is crucial in friendship because when we stop talking, problems arise. For example, your friend doesn't talk to you when you're walking down the hall. She sees you talking to someone else and keeps walking. Your friend didn't want to interrupt your conversation, but you think she's angry because you were talking to someone else. The next time you see her in the hall, you intentionally ignore her. She's hurt by your attitude, and now the walls are up. You don't talk to her at school, and you're certainly not calling her first. Now there's a misunderstanding on both sides. Your friend was just being respectful, but lack of communication shuts down the truth. Before long, you go for weeks without talking, other friends get involved, and the drama erupts. This scenario could have easily been resolved by asking your friend one simple question, "Were you upset with me when I saw you in the hall today?" Problem solved, drama over.

But what if your friend ignores you intentionally? While you're talking, she stares at her phone, rolls her eyes or looks at her watch. You feel disrespected and realize you're basically having a conversation with yourself. One-sided conversations are a killer in friendships. If you find yourself in a one-sided conversation, tell your friend you feel disrespected. You might say, "When you stare at your phone while I'm talking, I do not feel important to you." If your friend continues her behavior, stop talking and wait until she gives you her attention before continuing your conversation. You may also use a humorous approach. Say things that make no sense while you're talking with your friend and see how long it takes for her to catch on. When talking about school, you might say, "Yeah, today was a great day at school. We put our desks on top of the building while we were all wearing white and a whale landed on us." More than likely, your friend will pay attention. If she says, "What?" just laugh and tell her you want to be sure she's listening. She'll more than likely get the message.

"All about me" friends also shut down communication. If you've ever had an "all about me" friend, you know what I'm talking about. She only calls you to vent about HER problems, but when YOU have problems, she is nowhere around. If you find yourself on the receiving end of a friend's endless chatter about herself or her life, it can wear on your nerves quickly. To avoid further frustration, gently remind your friend that you'd like to talk about some things that are important to you, too. You may tell her, "You only call when you need to vent, but I'd like to talk when things are going *well* for you, too." If she changes, you've been heard. If she continues to talk only about herself over a period of time, you might want to reconsider the friendship. Someone who is only interested in talking about themselves usually doesn't make for a very good friend.

If YOU are the one who does more talking than listening in the relationship, be responsible. Acknowledge that your persistent talking may be annoying to your friend. Apologize, and let your friend know that you're interested in her life too, by asking, "How was your day?" "What's going on?" or, "What's the latest?" Let your friend know that you are genuinely interested in what's happening in HER life. One-sided friendships are not fun for anyone.

If you have difficulty knowing if you're in a one-sided friendship, this exercise may help. Take a piece of paper, draw a line down the middle, and write your name and your friend's name across the top. Next, write down all the contributions you feel you make to the friendship under your name. Then, do the same for your friend. You can quickly see if one of you is doing most of the giving. While giving to friends is good, being a doormat is not.

Silence is also a helpful form of communication in friendship. Silence can help us gain perspective on situations and help us handle things responsibly. The key is to limit your silence. As we saw with the example of the girls in the hallway, too much silence leads to suspicion. Let your friend know you need some time away if you are upset with her, but be sure to schedule a time to come back and talk about the issue. Disagreements in a friendship are normal, but make them count toward bettering your friendship. If you find that you were wrong in the situation, apologize. Colossians 3:13 reminds us that we must forgive others as Christ forgives us. Forgiveness means making a conscious choice to let go of the hurt that others cause us. While it is not easy, it is worth it. When we hold onto bitterness or anger, it's like taking

> *Silence can help us gain perspective on situations and help us handle things responsibly.*

poison and hoping the other person dies. When we forgive someone, we refuse to think about the damage they have done to us. We no longer allow them to "rent space in our head" because chances are good, they are out having a good time and they don't even know we are upset. Furthermore, they may not care that we are upset! This can be a process, but it's worth it. Forgiveness does not mean we must continue to have a relationship with someone who has hurt us. It means that we set them free from our thoughts so that they no longer control us. If you want to make the friendship work after you have been hurt, you must forgive.

Silence can also be lethal to friendships. We often pretend things don't bother us when they really do. When friends gossip about others, we may stay silent for fear of rejection if we disagree. We stay silent when hurtful, demeaning or bad language is used. We stay silent when we want to scream, "Stop hurting me, leave me alone, stop picking on me, stop embarrassing me, and stop gossiping." Instead, we just... stay... silent. When we're silent about pain in our friendship, problems can overwhelm us.

Shelly's "friend" Sam enjoys verbally stabbing her. Sam tells Shelly her teeth are too big. Shelly laughs, but inside she's ashamed. In the same conversation, Sam tells Shelly that no guy would want to kiss her "big ol' mouth." Sam laughs and says, "Just kidding," but the damage is done. Shelly hangs up the phone and cries. She looks in the mirror and wonders why God made her so ugly.

If Shelly remains silent, she teaches Sam that it's acceptable to verbally assault her. Shelly MUST speak up. Her conversation with Sam may sound something like the following: "You know Sam, we were talking on the phone the other day and you made the comment that my teeth were too big. You also said no guy would want to kiss my big mouth. I know you laughed, but it really hurt my feelings. I know my teeth are big, but I also believe the right guy will want to kiss me anyway. Please don't make fun of how I look anymore." The responsibility has now shifted to Sam. Shelly can do two things: wait and see if Sam apologizes, or make a decision to continue the friendship based on Sam's response. While Shelly is not responsible for Sam's actions, she is responsible for setting boundaries with Sam to avoid being mistreated in the future.

Sometimes silence is a gift to friends. Friends can get on our nerves, but if their behavior is not life threatening or abusive, it is often best to stay silent. When a friend picks her teeth with a knife in public, it may not be appealing, but it's not a deal breaker. Stay silent, and overlook your friend's annoying behavior. After all, the Bible reminds us that "love covers a multitude of sins" in 1 Peter 4:8. Sometimes, we simply have to overlook obnoxious behavior in our friends. They may just have to do the same for us

> *Above all, love each other deeply, because love covers over a multitude of sins. 1 Peter 4:8*

some day.

If your friend's behavior is obnoxious and selfish, silence may not be the answer. Christy and her friends enjoy studying together. They are straight-A students and take their grades seriously. Their friend Blair is in the study group, but jokes and laughs excessively during their study time. When Blair missed the main points of the discussion due to joking around and asks the group for help, Christy draws a healthy boundary. Christy tells Blair that they cannot repeat the information she missed due to the time limitations they have during study group. Christy encourages her to pay closer attention in the future to avoid missing information during study time.

Friend drama is one thing all the girls in our study group said they try to avoid. But what can you do when it happens? After all, friends have problems and we want to be there to help them. Becky and Lisa give us a good example. Becky called Lisa constantly about problems with her mom. Lisa wanted to help and really felt sorry for Becky. She listened to Becky, encouraged Becky, and even cried with her. Unfortunately, the calls kept getting worse instead of better. The more Lisa tried to help, the more Becky relied on Lisa for advice. Lisa became worried and even a bit depressed as a result. Lisa had to talk with Becky and put an end to the drama since it was now affecting both of them. Lisa told Becky she was sorry she was going through a difficult time with her mom, but she didn't know what else she could do to help. Lisa drew a healthy boundary with Becky and let her know that they would no longer be able to talk about her mom. Becky understood, and their friendship was stronger as a result. Had Becky not respected Lisa's boundary, trust would have been broken and their friendship may have ended.

Trust is a key characteristic in friendship.

Trust is a key characteristic in friendship. Trustworthy friends inspire you to be your best, encourage you in your walk with God, and remind you that you are loved no matter what happens. They inspire you to be all you can be, push you to dream big, and cheer you on while you reach your goals. Trustworthy friends understand your moods, excuse your bad days, and strive to influence you in a Godly way. Trustworthy friends are honest in their opinions, help guide you into making the best decisions, and show respect when your opinion or decisions are different from theirs. They work at making friendships last and help build memories that will last a lifetime.

Without trust in friendship, we can't be ourselves. We put on airs, pretend to be someone we're not, and friendship is awkward. We may be controlled or dependent on someone who doesn't care about us. We can also allow ourselves to be controlled by someone who really DOES care about us. For example, your friend adores you, but she tells you who you should and shouldn't date. You know she cares about you, so you feel guilty if you don't "obey" what she thinks is right.

She now has power over you, but you have willingly given it to her. Just because friends love us, they don't always know what is best for us. Praying and asking God's direction about our choices will always keep us from being controlled by even the most loving of friends.

Without trust in friendship, we may be dominated, gossiped about, or get left out. We're pushed into things we're uncomfortable with, we are lied about, and others lie to us. For example, let's say your friend continually flirts with your boyfriend. You have to confront her before it gets out of hand and when you do, she tells you, "There's nothing to it." She continues to flirt, so you end the friendship. Your boyfriend agrees that her flirting was risky and you wonder how you ever became friends in the first place!

Negative peer pressure can break trust in friendship. Proverbs 13:20 says, "Walk with the wise and become wise, for a companion of fools suffers harm." Many times we believe it is okay for us to do things simply because our friends are doing them. After all, we look up to them and respect them. We believe they have our best interest at heart, so why shouldn't we follow what they're doing? A real but difficult truth to accept is that friends DON'T always have our best interest at heart. When a friend tells you that you should steal from the store because they've never been caught, they don't have your best interest at heart. When they lie about you behind your back, they are not true friends, no matter what they say to your face.

When friends break our trust it hurts, but it doesn't always mean we have to end the friendship. Each situation is different and we must try to resolve our differences if at all possible. Romans 12:18 reminds us to do all that we can to live in peace with others.

In the following scenarios, how would you respond? Keep in mind, the goal is to restore the friendship because true friends are hard to find. Answer the following:

1. You have a birthday party coming up on Friday and your friend finds out your boyfriend has plans to break up with you the following Saturday. She doesn't tell you until after the party is over because she didn't want to ruin your party. Do you:

   a. Write your friend off?

   b. Thank her for saving your heart from being hurt until the party was over?

2. Your friend invites some friends over for dinner, but she doesn't invite you. She knows you don't like one of the girls who is coming, and doesn't want to make you feel uncomfortable. Do you:

   a. Get mad at your friend for not inviting you for dinner?

   b. Thank her for saving you from bad company?

Keeping a friendship through thick and thin is crucial. Our study group believes the following are important reminders if you want to have a solid friendship:

* Be honest. While everything doesn't have to be said, there are some things that must be said.

* Be a good listener. No one wants to hear someone continually talk about themselves.

* Speak kindly. Avoid words of gossip or offense.

* Be a giver. Help your friend with a project or pray them through a tough time.

* Have fun. If strife fills most of your time together, re-evaluate.

* Compromise. Friendship is give and take.

* Quickly forgive. No one is perfect.

* Be a good influence.

* Boys come and boys go, but friends are there to stay. Never let a boy come between you and a friend.

* Choose your words and actions wisely. You may be the only person your friend trusts.

* Maintain boundaries. Take a stand for those things that are most important to you and refuse to compromise.

> *The best friends to have are those that know everything about us and still love us anyway.*

Romans 12:10 reminds us that we should "honor one another above ourselves" because real friendships are a gift. The best friends to have are those that know everything about us and still love us anyway.

Reflection:

> ➢ What do you do when you feel ignored by a friend?

> ➢ Have you had a misunderstanding with a friend because of poor communication? What happened and how did you handle it?

> ➢ Is there a friendship in your life that is "one-sided?" What do you need to do to bring balance to this situation?

> ➢ Have you ever stayed silent with a friend when you wanted to speak up? Why?

> ➢ Have you confronted a friend who was hurtful? If so, are you still friends?

> ➢ If you had to confront a friend, what are some things that you might say?

CHAPTER FOUR

God-esteem

"Lift up your head princess. If not, the crown falls."
—*Unknown*

When talking with the teen girls in our study group, they all expressed concern about self-esteem. When it comes to esteem, we all want it, and God designed us to have it.

According to Webster, esteem is "admiration or respect." The term "self-esteem" is popular, but what if we can't have "*self*-esteem?" Before you think I'm crazy, let me explain. When we look to ourselves for esteem, we look to things that are temporary and can never really make us happy. For example, we cut our hair or date the "right" guy, and think that will give us esteem. We buy the right outfit or have the right friends, and think THAT will fix the problem. There's STILL a problem. When we look to temporary fixes as a permanent solution, we put our esteem in the hands of something or someone who is always changing. When we get tired of our hair, or break up with a guy, or get left out of the group, our esteem takes a nose dive. So where can we get esteem? Glad you asked. It can only be found in one place: God.

God NEVER changes!

God NEVER changes! No matter how you feel, how your hair looks, who you date or what you wear, He can never love you more than He does right now. You see, your heart is the "throne" of your life. When you allow God to sit on the throne of your heart, you give Him permission to bring "*God*-esteem" into your life. "God-esteem" will take you places, but when we try to do things without asking God to get involved, we eventually make a mess that takes us to places we don't want to go.

Cutting:

What are some areas where a lack of "God-esteem" shows up? Let's explore a few, beginning with cutting.

Most people have no idea why "cutters" cut. While "cutting" is NEVER the answer to life's pain, I do understand it. I had a close encounter with a "cutter" for years.

I counseled a girl I will call "Wendy" from the time she was nine until she stopped cutting at age 22. Wendy used everything imaginable to cut. She was often compared to her sister, and was blamed for everything bad that happened in her family. Eventually, she couldn't bear the pain of hearing how terrible she was, and began cutting. For years, my heart broke for her. I prayed for her, cried with her, and allowed her to use my home as an escape. I could see the pain she tried to release each time she cut and the fear she experienced when she cut too deep. She was in and out of hospitals several times, and was given many different medications. Nothing made her stop cutting.

Eventually Wendy grew tired of cutting. She made a choice to believe the truth of what God's Word said about her over the negative and hurtful screams she heard from home. She also discovered that she was NOT the cause for all of the problems in her family. The shame she carried for years eventually melted away and "God-esteem" took over. Wendy graduated from high school and earned both a Bachelor's and Master's Degree. Wendy's parents eventually divorced, and she was able to see that she had been carrying pain that was not hers to carry. I would tell you the awesome things she is doing with her life now, but you would recognize her identity. If you come to an "In Her Shoes" mother/daughter conference, you might just meet her.

"Cutters" cut for different reasons. Some cut because they're numb and want to feel something. Others cut because they are hurting and it's a way for them to get some form of temporary relief from the pain inside. For a lot of us, "cutting" makes no sense. Why would anyone want to intentionally hurt themselves? I can't even stand getting a shot! In order to understand the way Wendy thought, I had to really do my homework. I found that Wendy's world wasn't so far from mine. We all do things to avoid pain, shame, self-hatred or guilt. I often listen to music or call a friend to temporarily escape pain or things that are hard. Wendy was also avoiding pain, just in a different way. The difference? My solutions won't kill you; cutting can.

If you're a cutter, let me first say that you're not alone and there are those who can help you walk this road. Find someone you trust and talk with them. If you have not met a counselor you trust, find a trustworthy adult who understands cutting, or is willing to learn, and can hold you accountable when you get the urge to cut. Friends can help, but they often lack the coping skills needed. A trusted adult is a *must* in the life of a cutter.

If you are a cutter and you get the urge to cut, consider the following:

* Be aware of your triggers. What makes you want to cut? Avoid that situation or have a plan in place if you must face it.

* If you feel empty, focus on breathing, list the uses for a random object, bite into a lemon or stomp your feet on the ground.

* Put off the urge to cut. Instead of cutting, do something different until the urge passes. Call a friend, play with a pet, go for a run or walk, or take a shower (make sure there is nothing you can cut with in the bathroom or shower). I strongly suggest you CALL A TRUSTED ADULT. This is a good place to start on this step. Many times, Wendy and I were able to talk through her pain and she was able to stop

herself from cutting. If you can't reach your trusted adult, keep trying until you reach them. Be sure that your trusted adult understands the importance of being available when you need them. This is a sacrifice on their part, but they do it because they believe your life is worth it! They may not be available immediately each time you call, but find a trusted adult who does their best to get back with you as soon as they are able. Again, your trusted adult is someone you feel safe with, do not feel judged by, and is willing to learn and understand the dynamics of cutting.

* If you must feel pain, do something that isn't invasive. Snap your arm with a rubber band. Wear it on your wrist all day so you always have it with you. Draw red all over your arm with a marker (soft tip), or draw red all over a piece of paper. You can also use red paint and even let it dribble if that feels better. Draw out your pain on paper and share it with someone you trust. You may also rub an ice cube on your arm.

* If anger is what makes you want to cut, grab a stress ball or a ball of play dough and squeeze it or throw it. You may also choose to do strenuous exercise that doesn't hurt you, but makes you tired so you can relax. Tearing up blank pieces of paper may be helpful, or you may even choose to go outside and scream. The

neighbors may think you're weird, but that's
better than hurting yourself.

The most important thing to remember if you have
chosen to "cut" or self-injure is that you CAN stop.
There IS help. God did not design you to be a punching
bag at anyone's hands, especially your own. It IS your
choice, and YOU can be the one to be in control of this
area of your life. If you are reading this book and you
self-injure, reach out to your trusted adult and allow
them to help you find the answers you need.

What if you are not the cutter, but the friend of a cutter?
The following are some things you can do:

* You alone cannot solve the situation. You can
  listen, but a trusted professional needs to be
  involved. Don't beat yourself up if you can't get
  your friend to stop cutting. This is a serious
  issue that requires professional intervention.

* Let your friend know that you are there to listen.
  After asking about the cuts, your friend may or
  may not talk with you. Let them know the offer
  stands and that you are there for them when
  they're ready to talk.

* If your friend asks you not to tell, let them know
  you can't keep that promise because you care
  about them. Tell an adult you know who cares
  about your friend and can help. Parents,
  coaches, youth directors, teachers and
  counselors may be good options. Don't be

afraid to tell! Statistics show that 90% of cutters who receive treatment get better after one year (Lyness). Your friend may be mad at first, but you could help save her life! She will eventually thank you.

* Use sensitive words with your friend who cuts. For example, "I know you are going through so much... no wonder you feel so much pain." Avoid words like, "But you have such nice parents and they make good money." Cutters need empathy, not accusation.

* Encourage your friend to talk with others who can support them and get the help they need.

* Be a good example of dealing with pain. Model good coping skills when you face pain of your own instead of dwelling on the negative and complaining.

* Don't give them an ultimatum like, "I won't be your friend if you continue to cut." Let your friend know you will be there and continue encouraging them to get the help they need.

* Most importantly, DO NOT JOIN IN! Don't allow anyone to encourage you to cut to see how it feels. If they do, then you have a good reason to separate yourself from them. Never allow anyone to talk you into something you know is wrong for you.

Eating Disorders:
Another place we need "God-esteem" is in the mirror!
Many of us look in the mirror and say things to
ourselves we would *never* say to someone else. "You
look disgusting," may be something we say to ourselves,
but we would NEVER say that to any of our friends!
Why do we think it's ok to talk to ourselves like that?

Most of us can find something we don't like about
ourselves. I've done it, even as an adult.

I used to wonder why God didn't give me any lips.
Before you laugh, understand that lips were really
important during my generation. Julia Roberts was the
model for perfect lips and I felt like my lips were too
small. Since I wanted to look like Julia, I decided to do
something about it.

For one of my birthdays, I saved up enough money and
went to one of "those" doctors that could fix my face.
I had my lips injected with a filler that would instantly
give me bigger lips. They never told me how bad it
would hurt! When someone drives a six inch needle
into your mouth, it hurts! I tried to make the doctor
stop, but one of my lips was already injected, so we had
to do the other one or I would have been lopsided. I
cried when she stuck me again, and cried even harder
when they began bruising and swelling.

Some friends had planned a birthday party for me the
next day and I looked like I got hit by a truck. The funny
part? None of my friends said anything about my lips!
Oh, they noticed. When your lips are so big that they

walk into the room before you do, people notice. They didn't want to hurt my feelings, so everyone was quiet. I finally stood up in the middle of all my friends and through swollen, bruised lips said, "I got mythelf a wittle birfday pwesent yesterday. I bought me some wips." My lips were so swollen that I couldn't correctly say, "I got myself a little birthday present yesterday. I bought me some lips." They all started laughing and said, "Not notice? Of course we noticed!" We all laughed and I can tell you, I will never let someone put a needle in my lips again!

> **The price we pay to look good is high... too high.**

The price we pay to look good is high. Sometimes, it's too high. Those who battle eating disorders know how high the price can be.

Eating disorders occur when teens use food as a way to control other feelings in their lives. Anorexia nervosa is the extreme obsession and fear of gaining weight. Those with anorexia refuse to keep their weight at a healthy level, while others eat more than usual and then make themselves throw up. This is known as bulimia. Those with eating disorders often exercise excessively and try desperately to avoid the lies that tell them they are fat, ugly, and unacceptable.

So what is "normal eating?" Normal eating is more about our attitude toward food than it is how much or how little we eat. When we can eat without feeling guilty, stop eating when we are full and eat when we are hungry, we have a healthy outlook on eating. "Normal eating" is being hungry and grabbing a snack to keep you full until dinner. "Unhealthy eating" is being hungry, grabbing a snack, and then feeling guilty because now you feel "fat."

There are several signs that accompany those who struggle with anorexia, bulimia, binge eating disorder or compulsive overeating. If you struggle with one of the following, please immediately find a trusted adult you can confide in to express your concerns:

* You think and talk about food and dieting a lot.

* You know about the amount of energy (joules) in every type of food.

* You go into the bathroom after meals and make yourself get sick.

* You exercise for excessive amounts of time.

* Your weight changes (looking thin and continuing to lose weight or gaining a lot of weight).

* You feel a lot of shame about your body and being consumed with how you look.

* You are tired all the time and/or have poor concentration.

* You are always thinking about how you could be thinner.

* You eat when dealing with difficult emotions and then feel guilty afterward.

Most who struggle with eating disorders have very high expectations of themselves and are typically perfectionists. Television, magazines and the internet all try to tell us what "perfect" looks like. Unfortunately, we may begin to believe the lie that perfection really exists and begin to diet and exercise uncontrollably to try to reach perfection. Sadly, perfection never comes, and as we try harder to achieve it, we become ill in the process.

Those with eating disorders may also feel out of control in their life and try using food as a way to regain control. They may seem to be "together" on the outside, but feel badly about themselves on the inside. They may also have a difficult time telling others how they feel or what they need.

Whatever the cause, all eating disorders have one thing in common: they are very dangerous if left untreated. Those who go untreated eventually suffer terrible effects. Hip and joint pain (due to excessive exercise), a corroded esophagus and a raspy voice (from continual vomiting), missed periods, feeling cold all the time, loss of muscle tissue, irritability and sleeping problems are only a few of the effects when left untreated. If the illness is left untreated for an extended period of time, you may find yourself in the hospital. Some have even died from the effects of eating disorders.

If you struggle with an eating disorder, you are not alone and there is help. The lack of control, helplessness and self-loathing you feel does not have to continue. Tell a trusted adult that you are struggling with your thoughts about food. There is no shame in your feelings, but there is a truth that is missing in your life and your trusted adult can help you find it.

There is no shame in reaching out for help.

It is also a good idea to journal the voices that you are hearing inside your own mind about your weight. If you hear, "You're a fat pig," or "You're worthless," write it in a journal. Show your trusted adult the things that you continually hear about yourself and allow the adult in your life to speak truth to you in these areas. The truth is a first step on the road to recovery.

There is no shame in reaching out for help. School counselors, youth directors, pastors, Sunday school teachers, extended family or a friend's parents can help direct you to the support you need.

What if you have a friend who struggles with an eating disorder? The following are some suggestions you may want to keep in mind:

* Remind the person that you really care about them. If they seem angry that you mention their

eating disorder, continue to remind them how much you care about them.

* Contact a professional who can reach out to your friend. Trained professionals know how to reach your friend in ways that are helpful.

* Accept your friend for who they are, and do things with them just as you would have done before you recognized that they are struggling with the eating disorder.

* Tell your friend why you like having them as a friend.

* Don't talk about eating disorders all of the time. Attempt to talk about upbeat experiences with your friend more than talking about their illness.

* Don't talk about your own weight issues or dieting. Let your friend know you are there for them. If you need to talk about your own weight issues, find another friend to confide in.

There is help if you struggle with an eating disorder. Trust your doctor, friends and family to help you on your journey toward healing.

Alcohol and Drugs
The decision to use alcohol and drugs is one you will more than likely face during your teen years and God-esteem can help you make the right choices in this area.

Most of us have great friends with the same morals and values that we hold, but every now and then, we feel a "squeeze" when the group wants to do something that we know we shouldn't do. We know it as peer pressure. It sounds so cliché, but it happens to all of us.

When we feel like the "odd-ball" in the group, we often feel pressure to do things that we aren't comfortable doing. At some point, we'll make the choice of whether or not to drink alcohol, and how much of it we will drink. Let's face it, it's everywhere. Billboards, movies, videos, and TV give us the impression that it's part of everyday life and that everyone is doing it. NOT true. I'm not, and I know a lot of other people, including teens in our study group, who have made the choice to abstain from alcohol. Why would anyone want to do that? Let me give you some facts, then you decide.

The "National Clearinghouse for Alcohol and Drug Information" has published the following about teens and alcohol:

* Car crashes, murder and suicide are the three leading causes of death for those ages 15-24 and alcohol is a major contributor. Sadly, many of these deaths happen to the one who WASN'T drinking, but accompanied the one drinking at the time.

* 75% of rapes happen when at least one person is under the influence of alcohol.

* Dehydration, dulled senses, memory loss, weight gain, decreased reaction time and impaired judgment are all ways our body is affected when we use alcohol.

These are just a few facts, but let me give you one from the Bible. Ephesians 5:18 says, "Don't be drunk with wine, (any alcohol), because that will ruin your life. Instead, let the Holy Spirit fill and control you."

Why would the Bible say something like that? Because we can get stupid when we drink. We make decisions we can't take back, and some can be life-changing when we are under the influence of alcohol.

Think it will never happen to you? Neither did Lisa. Lisa threw a party at the age of 15 when her parents went out of town. Most at the party began binge drinking hard alcohol, including Lisa. She passed out and all Lisa remembers is waking up to disaster. Someone drove through Lisa's house with their car and did damage to her home. Lisa's friend was struck by the car and was paralyzed for life. The story doesn't stop there. When Lisa woke up, she was naked and her body had been drawn all over with marker. She didn't remember anything, but assumed she'd engaged in some type of sexual encounter. She really... didn't... know.

Lisa says the decision to drink so much that night haunts her every day of her life. She struggles daily to let go of the guilt she feels for her friend being paralyzed. Her parents no longer trust her and she's lost the right to stay alone when her parents are gone.

Lisa was a normal 15 year old who began experimenting with alcohol to escape some pressure she was feeling. After the party, Lisa realized, "I thought using alcohol would solve my problems. It only made them worse."

...one moment under the influence can change your life forever.

Sadly, that's not an unusual story. Like you, most teens believe, "It will never happen to me." Unfortunately, one moment under the influence can change your life forever.

You can still be fun and be the life of the party when you're NOT drinking. How do I know? I did it! I used to be accused of being the one who was drunk at a party, but I was completely sober! I could laugh and have fun without alcohol. I was not so insecure that I felt like I had to have a drink in my hand to fit in. You can do the same.

Another thing I loved about being the one who didn't drink at parties was that others didn't pressure me, they took up for me! When someone asked me if I wanted a drink, my friends would say, "Leave her alone! She doesn't drink." Cool! The ones offering me the drink were being pressured, not me.

Do you want to stand out and get attention? This is a great way to do it. Be fun, be lively, but be sober! Find friends who support your decision to remain sober and hang with them. You won't regret it and all you're missing out on is a hangover. The best part? You'll remember everything that happened the next day!

So what if no one at the party has your back? Here are some things you can say when offered a drink:

* "No thanks, I'm driving."

* "No thanks, I'm not into drinking."

* "No thanks, I don't drink."

* "No thanks, I have a lot going on tomorrow and I need to be on my game."

If someone doesn't have enough respect for your choices and keeps pressuring you, ditch them and find someone else to hang out with. Chances are good they've already had too much to drink and won't remember talking to you anyway. You may also choose to leave the party.

Drugs are another area where we must make choices using God-esteem.

Unfortunately, it is easy for teens to make and buy drugs. Why do they need them? The answer is simple. There's some hole, pain or stress in their life that they want to numb, so they turn to this garbage. Yeah, I said it. It's garbage. Many teens have no idea, nor care, what drugs can do to their minds and bodies. All they care about is forgetting their pain for a while when they get high. The problem is that their issues are still going to be there when they come down. Sometimes, their problems are worse, depending on what they did while they were high. This is not a fun way to live.

Teens who are desperate to get high will go to great lengths to get drugs. OTC (over the counter drug) use is at an all-time high. Everything from cough syrup to allergy medicine is being misused. I must admit, it is really irritating when I have to show my driver's license to buy Sudafed (allergy medicine) because others are using it to make drugs.

Prescription and illegal drugs are also being abused by many. Bath salts, meth, cocaine, prescription anti-depressants, pain medication, cough and cold medicine, marijuana, inhalants, heroin, spice, even tobacco and nicotine are just some of the things teens are using to cause life-altering damage. Some die at an early age due to drug use.

So what's your part? First, decide where you stand. Say, "No!" and mean it! Learn coping skills that have long-term effects so that you're not tempted by the short-term effects of taking drugs.

Say, "No!" and mean it!

Teens take drugs to mask pain, fight low self-esteem, fit in, and because they're easily accessible. They love the short-term feeling drugs offer, but when the effect wears off, they need more to stay "fixed." Before long, they're addicted. Don't want to get caught up in that drama? Learn to conquer stress instead of giving in to drugs. Here are some options:

* Do not expect to be perfect. Having high expectations of yourself is fine, but pressure on yourself to be perfect is unrealistic.

* Simplify. Do not allow your schedule to put you on overload. Learn to say, "No" to things that you don't *have* to do.

* Include healthy, stress-free activities in your life that you enjoy, like running, dancing, hanging out with friends, reading a great book or listening to music you love.

* Find trusted friends and/or adults that you can talk with about problems.

* If you feel like you need an adrenaline rush for excitement, participate in extreme sports or get involved in an organization you're passionate about.

ask God to fill the hole that is there with the "high" only He can give.

God is able to give you a "high" that no drug can offer. When the need for "something more" comes up in your life, ask God to fill the hole that is there with the "high" only He can give. No drugs or alcohol are needed.

Gender Identity:
Another area where "God-esteem" must live is in our gender identity. I dare to tackle this topic because you are more than likely going to have friends or classmates who may struggle with gender identity and an attraction to the same sex. God's Word is clear on this topic and as Christians, we need to know how to interact with those who are struggling in a helpful, non-combative way.

We are never to excuse sin of any kind, and God is very clear that he hates the sin of homosexuality. He loves the people, but He is very outspoken against homosexuality in both the Old and New Testaments. You can read more in Deuteronomy 23:17, Leviticus 18:22, and Ephesians 5:5, to name a few. To those who may see my words as "biased," be careful how you judge. I walked through one of the most difficult seasons of my life as I watched my closest cousin struggle with his gender identity and eventually die at a young age because of the choices he made. When we choose to keep self on the throne instead of allowing God to live there, the consequences are serious.

Choices are life-changing.

I have also seen those I love move out of homosexuality and courageously live the life God has called them to live. Choices are life-changing.

A friend of mine, we'll call Mary, went to her youth director when she was in junior high school, admitting same-sex attraction. Mary got what others have experienced: rejection. Mary was shamed for her feelings and as a result, believed she was inherently flawed. She left the church, acted on her same-sex attraction and eventually became engaged to her partner. She eventually purchased a gay bar and was very involved in the homosexual lifestyle. She had no desire to live any differently.

I was teaching a women's conference the first time I met Mary. She was very skeptical of what the church would think of her being there, and what I would think of her being there. Many at the conference knew Mary's struggle, but they chose to love Mary instead of reject her. I did the same. Because of my experience with my cousin, I knew unconditional love was the first thing she needed. After all, that's what Jesus would have done, right? I did NOT love her sin, but I did love HER.

After the conference, I asked Mary this question: "How has the church failed you?" She looked at me with hesitation and said, "I tried to be honest, and the church rejected me." I told her that I was sorry for the rejection that she had experienced and that I loved her. She looked at me like I had three heads. She wondered how I could love her if I didn't even know her! I could do that because I knew Jesus loved her.

As a result of God changing Mary's heart at that conference, she asked Jesus to sit on the throne of her heart. She broke off her engagement with her partner, sold her gay bar and began a new life. That's what happens when we love people, speak the truth of what God's Word says to them in love, and let God do the rest.

Our friends may struggle with same-sex attraction, but we can't leave them there. God has more for their life, and we have to show them! You may say, "But they don't think they're in a mess, Ms. Shannon. They like what they're doing." Mary said the same thing until God got on the throne of her heart. Change is possible.

If you have a friend or classmate who struggles with same-sex attraction, be courageous enough to speak the truth in love. You can offer truth without being "preachy" by sharing the following:

* Remind them that God loves them unconditionally even when they have experienced rejection by others (John 3:16-1; John 3:1-3).

* Show them the same love that Christ would show them. Jesus hated sin, not sinners. We can show love to others without approving of what they do.

* Be willing to share what God's Word says about all sexual sin. Remind them that God loves them, but that He hates all sexual sin, and homosexual sin is included. Romans 1:18-32, I Corinthians 6:9-11 and I Timothy 1:9-11 are good verses to share. They may not change their mind immediately after reading those

Scriptures, but the truth is what sets people free. It's our job to share the truth. It's God's job to do the changing.

It's our job to share the truth. It's God's job to do the changing.

* Suggest that your friend talk to a trusted Christian counselor or another trusted adult who can talk about the issues they're facing. Sometimes, those who have been abused or abandoned struggle with same-sex attraction until those deeper issues have been resolved.

* Be sure that YOU talk with a trusted adult to make sure you are handling the situation in the best way possible.

* Pray for your friend. We all struggle with sin and we all need forgiveness. God designed your friend as a male or female ON PURPOSE. Pray that they are able to have a new identify in Christ and leave behind the confusion that comes with same-sex attraction.

If you're struggling with same-sex attraction, let me be the first to say, "I'm sorry if you have been hurt or abused by others, especially in the church." Many times, people don't know how to appropriately respond to things they don't understand.

The truth is, God loves you and He has an amazing plan for your life. He created you as female (or male if you're reading this and you're a guy) on purpose. He is SO happy with how He created you and He wants to lovingly show you why He chose you to be that way. He also understands that we all struggle, so He provides a way out of the torment and confusing thoughts and emotions that you may face.

There are those who understand where you are. Dennis Jernigan shares one of the most powerful same-sex attraction stories I have ever heard and I highly encourage you to read it. You can find his story and many other resources when you check out his website, dennisjernigan.com. Dennis has been there, and understands the struggle you are facing. His same-sex attraction took him to the brink of suicide before God got on the throne of his life. There is a way out. "God-esteem" is yours for the taking.

Reflection:

➢ Do you know anyone who "cuts" or self-injures? If so, what has been most helpful when talking with them?

➢ Have you ever been tempted to "cut" or "self-injure?" If so, why and how did you stop?

➢ If you are currently self-injuring, how will you reach out for help?

➢ Have you struggled with an eating disorder or known those who have? If so, what have you learned as a result?

➢ If you currently struggle with an eating disorder, what has been most helpful for you? Most hurtful?

➢ How can teens overcome the pressure to use alcohol and drugs?

➢ What role should parents play in their teen's life where alcohol and drugs are concerned?

➢ Do you know someone with an addiction to drugs or alcohol? What are the negative effects of addiction?

➢ What will YOU do if you are offered drugs or alcohol?

➢ How do you approach those who struggle with gender identity? Do you tend to address the issue or leave it alone?

➢ When talking with someone who struggles with their gender, how can you stand for truth without being judgmental?

➢ If you struggle with gender identity, who can you trust to talk with about your thoughts/feelings?

CHAPTER FIVE

Beating the Bullies

"Your value doesn't decrease based on someone's inability to see your worth."

—*Unknown*

Idiot. Ugly. Fat. Loser. For most of us, nothing is more painful than rejection. We may say it doesn't bother us, but rejection plays with our mind and fights to make us believe its lies.

People who are hurt often hurt others. Bullies fall into this category. A lot of times we think of bullies as people who say mean words, but bullies can be as equally hurtful when they say nothing and ignore us.

Bullies hurt others because they have a need for control. Something in their life is out of control, so they find others they PERCEIVE as weaker to belittle and control. When a bully finds a person who is different from them in some way, they automatically treat that difference as a weakness. Then, they attack.

Bullies feed on their victim's reactions such as hurt, fear, insecurity and weakness. If the victim doesn't react in

> Bullies feed on their victim's reactions such as hurt, fear, insecurity and weakness.

these ways, the bullying often gets worse until they get the reaction they want. Somehow, they feel better about themselves when they hurt someone. You may be thinking, "Why would anyone feel better about themselves after knowingly hurting someone?" The bully's sole purpose is to get a reaction out of the one they are bullying. When they do, they believe they have gained control and that they "win." This makes them feel better about themselves for a while, but then they bully again.

So how would you respond to a bully? Read the following scenarios, then decide what YOU believe would be the best way to deal with the bully in each situation.

Situation 1:
Carrie and Amy have been best friends since elementary school, but when they got into high school, things changed. Amy began hanging out with some "mean" girls. Carrie really values Amy's friendship and it is hurting her to watch Amy get caught up in the wrong crowd. The "mean" girls begin picking on Carrie. Amy really doesn't like it, but she doesn't stand up for Carrie and as a result, Carrie is very hurt. When Carrie talks with Amy, she apologizes and even cries, saying it won't

happen again. Unfortunately, it does happen again and Amy is silent to Carrie's feelings one more time.

Carrie should:

    a. End her friendship with Amy.

    b. Ask Amy to make a choice between her and the "mean" girls.

    c. Talk to the "mean" girls and tell them to stop picking on her.

    d. Stay friends with Amy and say nothing.

Many times, we can't see how badly we're being treated until we back away from a situation. It is very hard to do when emotions are involved, so in the situation above, being alone for a few days to reflect may be best. In this situation, it might be helpful to grab a piece of paper and draw a line down the middle. List the advantages of the friendship on one side, and the negatives on another. You may find that in the beginning of the friendship, there were a lot of positives, but now, it brings more hurt feelings than good ones. If you choose to put distance between you and your friend by not speaking to her for a while, she may eventually realize what she has lost and decide to leave the "mean" girls behind. If she does not, your friend is probably in for a lot of trouble. If the girls were mean to you, they will eventually be mean to your friend. Even worse, she may become like them. Either way, it will not be a good situation.

Situation 2:

You're dating a boy who is always putting you down. He says that he's joking, and he even makes you laugh about it sometimes. After all, they're only words. At first it doesn't bother you, but slowly, you begin to feel like you ARE the things he's telling you. You really care about this guy, and he's not mean to anyone else but you. You begin to believe you *must* be the problem. Eventually, he doesn't just talk in a mean way; he begins telling you that you can't be with your friends unless he's around. You used to spend time laughing and talking with your friends, but lately it seems like they don't come around much anymore. You don't want to lose him, but you don't want to lose your friends either.

Do you:

a. Break up with him and tell him to "hit the road?"

b. Stay with him and watch all your friendships disappear?

c. Tell him what's bothering you and let him know you are done with the relationship if he doesn't stop?

d. Ask for guidance from an adult you trust?

When we are "in love" or even like a guy, sometimes our thinking can get weird. We let them talk us into doing things we know are wrong, talk to us in ways that are degrading and hurtful, or even give up boundaries we have because they say they are doing everything in the name of "love." Bullies often hide their behavior from others until they feel they have control. They may treat you great in the beginning of your relationship then suddenly, and without warning, throw words at you that hurt. They tell you, "You're too sensitive," and you should, "Get over it." They tell you something is wrong with *you*. In reality, there is something very wrong with THEM. Guys who like to control girls do so because they have the "ideal" girl in their head. If you don't match their "fantasy girl," they will belittle and control you until you become what they want. The problem? They are never satisfied. They will always want more and you can never please them.

If you find yourself dating a guy who is a bully, you will need to confront him-and waste no time doing it. Let him know that his behavior is hurtful and you will not allow him to treat you in a way that is less than what you deserve. Set limits when he bullies you by saying, "Stop it," disagreeing with him, or walking away. Let him know that there are consequences if his behavior does not change, and one of those may be the loss of the relationship. Explain that he needs to consider your feelings and thoughts on things. Take the scenario above, for example. If you were in this situation, let him

God did not design us to be mistreated or bullied.

know that he is important, but so are your friends. Guys often come and go, but friendships last when they are nurtured. If a guy bullies you and tells you that you have to dump your trusted friends to keep him around, kick him to the curb and keep your friends! They will be there to care about you as you move on to the next guy who treats you the way you should be treated. If you are unsure about how to handle a bully that you are dating, talk with a trusted adult who can help.

God did not design us to be mistreated or bullied. In both of the scenarios above, ask God to show you what to do and for the courage to do it. He will.

While handling bullies face to face is tough, cyberbullying offers a whole new set of challenges. Cyberbullying takes place when someone bullies you through technology. Boys tend to cyberbully differently from girls. Guys usually cyberbully by "sexting" or threatening physical harm, while girls spread rumors and lies to make others think badly about you. They may also leave you out of groups or messages online to intentionally exclude you. Cyberbullies can torment us 24 hours a day if they have a mobile device or computer and this often makes us feel unsafe wherever we go, even in our own home!

If you are a victim of cyberbullying, it is most important to know that you are NOT alone. Over half (52 percent) of young people report being cyber bullied. ("Cyber Bullying Statistics 2014") The good news is, you don't have to tolerate it. There are ways to stop cyberbullying.

First of all, NEVER respond to a cyberbully. A reaction is what they want, so no matter how tempted you are, DO NOT RESPOND. If you do, the bullying will get worse. By not responding, you have the power to show the bully that you will not allow yourself to be intimidated. If they continue to bully you, take the next step.

Collect all evidence of cyberbullying on a flash drive and report it to your internet service provider immediately! Allow your parents to help you do this. By storing the evidence, you are taking control of the situation in a mature and healthy way. Too many times, teens retaliate and become cyberbullies themselves. Don't stoop to a bully's level by responding. Store it, and put your focus on things that make you feel good and bring you happiness.

If you are being cyberbullied, be sure to tell an adult you trust who will listen and take action. Too many times, teens are afraid to ask for help because the bully threatens that they will bully more if someone tells on them. NEVER allow a cyberbully to "brainwash" you into protecting them or believing their lies. Expose them for what they are and stand up for what is right.

Be sure you also block the cyberbully from being able to talk with you online. If you don't know how to block a bully, ask a trusted adult to help you. If you find yourself being "chased" online by the bully each time they are blocked, you need to decide where you want to hang out online. For example, if you are bullied on

Instagram, it would be wise to stay off Instagram for a while. WHERE you "live" online is important.

If a bully taunts you, try ignoring them. They are trying to get a reaction from you so that they can gain control. Some bullies will stop bullying when you ignore them, but some will see it as a challenge and will bully even more. If so, you may need to confront the bully. While this can be scary, it is often what shuts them down.

We teach other people how to treat us.

When confronting a bully, be sure you do so with confidence, assurance, and in a calm way. If you lose your composure and begin to cry or get angry, they will see you as weak. Let the bully know that you will not allow them to treat you in any way other than what you deserve. We teach other people how to treat us.

Let's take the following scenario. If "Sarah" is your bully, you may say something like, "Sarah, you made fun of the dress I was wearing when we were in homeroom last week. I like that dress and get a lot of compliments from others when I wear it. Maybe you don't like dresses, but I do. If you don't have something nice to say to me, you don't have to talk to me, but I would like for you to stop making fun of my clothes." Now, this can do one of two things. "Sarah" will feel embarrassed because you called her out, or she will see it as a challenge and will keep bullying. If she sees it as a challenge, stay away from "Sarah" or keep friends around who are supportive. If you have to be around her when friends are not around, let an adult know who will support you. You have the right to be safe at all costs.

You can also laugh at a bully. They really hate this, but it gets the point across in an awesome way! For example, a bully says, "You're so fat." Say something back like, "Hey, you're pretty observant. I have gained a few pounds lately, thanks for noticing." It will shut them down because it catches them off guard.

There are three roles to every bullying situation: the bully, the bullied, and the bystander. What if you're not the victim of bullying, but you are a bystander who is watching someone be bullied? If your friend or someone you know is being bullied, you play a powerful role in helping to bring bullying to an end. Unfortunately, bystanders sometimes choose not to get involved.

Why do we dread getting involved as a bystander to a bullying situation? Several reasons come to mind. First, we often fear retaliation. If we stand up against a bully, they may come after us! We may also fear what others will think of us if we stand up against the bully, especially when they're popular. If the bully is someone others like, we may even feel pressured to become a bully, hoping we can be popular too.

Recently, I read about a girl who was in high school and decided to stand up against a bully. Katy was smart and was scheduled to be valedictorian of her class. When Katy saw a new student at her school being bullied, she confronted the bully. Unfortunately, the bully turned on Katy. He spread rumors about her at school and she was severely cyberbullied at home each night. Eventually, the bullying became so bad that Katy had to leave her school and lost the opportunity to graduate as valedictorian of her class. When asked how she felt about not getting to graduate as valedictorian because she stood up to the bully, she said, "I would do the same thing all over again if I had the chance." Now THAT'S a girl I would want to be friends with, wouldn't you? It takes a lot of courage and a lot of character to do the right thing.

> Why should we get involved? Because most bullies fly under the radar of adults.

Why should we get involved? Because most bullies fly under the radar of adults. As a school counselor, I was often shocked at how long some bullying situations in our school had been going on before I was told about them. Some adults even brush bullying off as no big deal or a normal part of teen behavior. Unfortunately, bullying is often ignored until it's too late. That is what happened to my precious friend, Tara.

Tara was a student I had the privilege of counseling. She was vivacious, full of life, and a beautiful girl. She was also very sensitive to others and had a lot of friends. When we visited, we talked about her family, but mostly, we talked about kids who made fun of her. Tara became a victim of bullying in Kindergarten. Kindergarten! The bullying followed Tara through elementary school, and eventually into high school.

Tara was a member of the drill team in high school and was pretty, popular and friendly. She had a lot of friends, and was caring to all she knew. Unfortunately, several girls on the drill team saw Tara's sensitivity as weakness. Tara could never understand what she had done to "make" these girls dislike her. She tried to be friends with them, but they pursued her more. They made false accusations that broke Tara's spirit. She reported the bullying to her drill team teacher, but the bullying didn't stop. The school counselor was notified, but the bullying continued. The principal was even aware, but the bullying never stopped. Tara's mom did all she could to save her daughter, but the devastating effects of bullying took their toll. Tara abruptly ended her life at the age of 17.

I had the privilege and overwhelmingly difficult task of speaking at Tara's funeral. I will never forget what I saw when I stepped onto the stage of that church. Both the upper and lower levels were filled with teenagers who loved Tara. I believe if Tara could have seen all the love and support that day, she may not have taken her life. Unfortunately, that's the breakdown. We mourn the death of those who take their life because of bullying, but why don't we get involved BEFORE they do such a permanent thing? Some of the girls who knew that Tara was being bullied were so sorry they didn't help her, and they will live with their decision for a long time. I will always wonder how things may have been different if someone would have been courageous enough to stand up for her.

WE can be the difference when someone is being bullied. Let's fill the balcony of a victim's life by being their supporter so that we don't have to fill a balcony at their funeral. Let's drop the lame excuses that we make for not getting involved and be brave enough, and loving enough, to take a stand. After all, that's what Jesus did.

In John 8, there was a woman who was going to be stoned by a group of people because she had committed the sin of adultery. In those days, it was a popular form of punishment to kill someone by throwing stones at them until they died. Jesus came onto the scene and He made a very powerful statement to all those who were ready to kill her. He said, "He who is without sin, cast the first stone." One by one, they all dropped their rocks and walked away. Why? Because they knew in their hearts that they were as guilty as she was of doing wrong.

Bullies like to "throw stones" because it keeps the focus off of their flaws and weaknesses. The good news? We all have flaws and weaknesses, so that makes us equal.

God made us the way that we are on purpose, and for others to hurt us with bullying behavior is for them to say that God did a bad job with us. If God was smart enough to make the entire universe, He certainly knew what He was doing when He created you. HE didn't mess up! You are "fearfully and wonderfully made" according to Psalm 139:14, and God hates it when others are hurtful to you because He loves you and is proud of who you are. If a bully's words or actions can't be backed up by what the Bible says about you, then they are a lie! Bullies do not get to define us, GOD does.

Bullies do not get to define us, GOD does.

If you ever find yourself tempted to bully, or wonder if you exhibit bullying behavior, ask yourself the following questions:

*   Do you enjoy hurting others or making fun of them on purpose?

*   Do you enjoy the fact that others are afraid of you?

*   Do you blame others for your problems or believe that someone deserves your bullying?

If you answered "Yes" to any of the above questions, I encourage you to talk with your parents or another trusted adult. Chances are good that you have been hurt and you are longing to lash out because of the hurt you are carrying. Lashing out at others will only bring you more pain, so find someone you can talk with and avoid becoming a bully.

If we all join together and form an alliance against bullying we can stop it. Are you in?

This is Tara and her mom.

Reflection:

> ➤ Have you ever been a victim of bullying? If so, what happened and how did you handle it?

> ➤ Have you ever witnessed someone being bullied? What did you do?

> ➤ What can adults do to help when bullying takes place?

> ➤ Have you ever bullied someone? What made you want to bully?

> ➤ If you did bully someone, what made you want to stop? Have you stopped? If not, why not?

> ➤ Why do YOU believe bullying is wrong?

> ➤ What will you do the next time you see someone being bullied?

CHAPTER SIX

Talking So Parents Will Listen

"It's better to be the owner of your silence than the slave of your words."

—*Unknown*

Every teenager experiences it. It hits and you can't explain it. That "I don't feel like talking" moment comes over you and it's usually right when your parents *want* to talk, right? If you're like most teenagers, you've felt it at some point. Sometimes it feels like parents have a radar, and when you don't want to talk, that's when they ask the most questions. "How was your day?" "Are you friends with that girl? No? Why not?" The questions keep coming until you explode. You may yell, cry, or run to your room in frustration. You get grounded and lose your cell phone for being disrespectful and then feel worse! How can you talk with your parents so that you don't feel bad, don't hurt their feelings, and keep your cell phone all at the same time?

Contrary to popular belief, most parents are really not trying to drive their teens crazy. They're trying to connect with you. When they tell you how much they love you, they really mean it. That's why they want to know what's going on in your life. Most parents are not nosy or controlling (no eye rolls please). They know they only have a limited amount of time with you and they're doing their job! That's right. They have a job to do, and God is counting on them to do it. While some of your jobs may include cleaning your room, taking out the trash, or cleaning up after a pet, one of their top jobs is to be in your business. It's just what God designed them to do! Not to control, but to guide. One day, they will answer to God for how they did as a parent. You see, they hold you accountable, but they are also being held accountable for the kind of parenting job they're doing. We want our parents to be the best parents possible because, let's face it, it makes OUR lives easier. Isn't that great? We have the power to make our lives easier, or more difficult. It's all about our choices.

> **We have the power to make our lives easier, or more difficult.**

The first thing we have to understand is not something we all necessarily want to hear: parents ARE the boss of us. I know you may not like that one, but don't close the book just yet. Be open-minded enough to consider what I'm saying if you don't agree. They work hard to give us what we need. They let us live in their house, shower with their water, eat their food, and use their electricity. Most of us even get extra spending money, clothes, and shoes! You may think that's far-fetched, but that stuff belongs to whoever pays the bill. If that still doesn't make you feel grateful, take a walk around your town's homeless areas and see if they would trade places with you. I believe they would. Now, before you think I have completely jumped on the parent bandwagon, let me add that I know some of us have better living arrangements than others. I'm just asking you to focus on the things you DO have with parents.

Exodus 20:12 says, "Honor your father and mother so that you may live long in the land the Lord your God is giving you." If you want to live, you have to honor your parents. That includes the way you talk to them. These aren't my words, by the way. They are God's words and they were written for every teenager who has ever lived even back in the day of Moses!

If we want to be able to talk to our parents, we need to look at what kind of communicator we are in the relationship. Some of us have an easier time opening up to our parents than others, so knowing *how* we communicate in the relationship will help.

The following are some different ways that teens communicate. Which one describes you?

➢ Passive – You worry about expressing yourself because of what others will think about you; you are afraid to say no for fear of making someone mad or you say, "I don't care!" when you really do.

➤ Aggressive – You don't care how what you say affects others as long as you get your way; you use harsh or hurtful words to intimidate so you get your way; your friends or parents are afraid of you.

➤ Passive-aggressive – You often say one thing but mean something different; you are reluctant to say anything when upset, but slam doors, pout, or give the silent treatment instead; you are sarcastic with others during a conversation.

➤ Assertive – You believe you have the right to express your thoughts and emotions and when you disagree with others, say what you feel or believe respectfully; you show respect during conversations and listen to others so that they know you are genuinely interested in their perspective.

In order to have productive and helpful conversations with your parents, the LAST one is the one you most want to be. If you struggle with being passive, aggressive or both, ask your friends how they see it negatively affecting you and how you could change. Chances are, they have heard you talk the same way to them if you've been friends very long. When you work to improve the way you talk with others, all of your relationships will improve, including the one with your parents.

Communication can make or break relationships, so the following are some important things to remember when having a conversation with your parents:

1. Your parents are a lot more like you than you realize. They were once teenagers, and as adults, they still have thoughts and feelings. Parents tend to receive most information much easier when you talk with them in a loving way. This is not the same as "buttering" them up. This is love from the heart, letting them know you value them as humans. Love is not a "feeling" alone, it's an action. You may not "feel" like showing love to your parents, especially when you disagree with them, but it is in your best interest when you do. If you struggle to show love to your parents, find at least one good quality in them or what they have done for you, and focus on it. Are they good listeners? Let them know you appreciate being heard. Do they work hard so they can make money to support you? Thank them for providing for you. This is the time when you wait on telling them what's wrong or what you're upset about, and focus on the one (and hopefully more) things that you love and appreciate about them. You don't like for your parents to judge you, so you must give them the same courtesy.

> Love is not a "feeling" alone, it's an action.

103

2. Another thing that will benefit you when talking to parents is to talk in language they understand. Your parents aren't hanging out at your school every day, and they don't always know the latest words you use. For example, parents go to the "bay" to fish while your "bae" is your crush (although I'm pretty sure this silly word should have never been invented). Talk to your parents with words that are respectful and that they understand. If you want or need something, be clear about what it is that you want and why that would be a good thing for your life. They may or may not agree with you, but if you are clear, they can give you an intelligent reason if the answer is, "No." Parents aren't mind readers, so be clear. Don't make them guess what you are trying to say, or you may miss out on something they would have done for you if they had understood what you wanted. Most importantly, communicate with respect. Curse words and attitudes don't belong in parent/teen relationships and they don't get you what you want in the long run.

3. We must also be truthful with parents. In case you haven't figured it out by now, telling the truth is always the best option. How many times have you known someone who told a half-truth, only to find out later they got into

> Learning to live a life of honesty will strengthen any relationship you have.

more trouble because they lied? My mom used to tell me, "If you tell me the truth, you may get into trouble, but it won't be nearly as bad as it would be if you lie." We have to be bold enough to tell the truth when we're confronted, even when it doesn't feel good. After all, our life is our responsibility. We have to start taking responsibility for all we tell our parents. Learning to live a life of honesty will strengthen any relationship you have.

Sometimes we do all of the above, but starting a conversation with parents is still awkward. The following are a few helpful ideas to keep in mind when you need to talk:

* Find a time that works well for you and for your parents. The more relaxed you both are, the better.

* Find a quiet area where there are no distractions.

* To begin the conversation, ask your parents about their day. They will appreciate the fact that you care about them and they are more likely to listen to what you have to say.

* Be clear if there is something specific you have to share, and if they react negatively to your

topic, don't react negatively in return. Stay calm and stay on topic.

* Allow your parents to have their say in the conversation without interrupting. Once they are finished, thank them for being willing to let you share what's on your mind.

* If you feel like you haven't been heard and still need to talk, thank them for listening to what you had to say, and ask them if there is another day you can talk about it when you are both calm.

When talking with parents, physical cues are just as important as verbal cues. For example, show your parents respect when you talk by looking them in the eyes. Don't give disgusted looks, squinted eyes or rolled eyes. Those conversations never end well.

Facial gestures can also be disrespectful. If you're not sure if you make disrespectful faces when talking to your parents, ask them. First, they will be shocked that you asked, but they will also tell you. Work on your facial expressions in the mirror. Practice some of the things that you will say to your parents and watch your face. If you make a face that you know your parents probably won't approve of, work on changing it. You can do it, and it will help make your life easier too.

So what happens when you disagree with your parents? Disagreements can actually be bridges that make the relationship better instead of dynamite that blows it apart. When you have a disagreement with your parents and need to solve a problem, try the following:

1. Define the problem. For example, if the disagreement is about the time of your curfew, calmly talk with your parents. If they have a set time in mind, allow them to explain their reasoning. If you don't understand their reasoning, respectfully ask for them to help you understand why your curfew can't be a later time. You must respect their rules, but they may be open to making exceptions for certain rules if you stay calm.

2. Attack the problem, not each other. Avoid sarcasm, threats and blame. Try to make sure that you understand what your parents are saying as you talk with them. You may say something like, "What I hear you saying is that you want me home by midnight because you are concerned about other drivers not being responsible." They do make the rules, but understanding *why* the rules are there can help you understand that they are coming from a direction of love, not control.

   a. If this step does not go as planned and you do feel like attacking your parents, excuse yourself and go to another room. Call a friend and talk through your anger and frustration about your parents. Talking with someone else will usually help you process what you would like to say to your parents and helps keep you from doing damage to your relationship. If a friend is not available to help you process your feelings, journal them in a notebook and share them with your friend at a later time.

b. If you DO explode and have an argument with your parents, take time away to calm down. People often say words they don't mean during the heat of an argument. Give each other some space to reflect on what was said, then come back together to discuss things when you are calm. While you take your space, write down the things that you got angry about and come up with a way to express that anger in a calm way. Your feelings are not right or wrong, but the way you express them can help heal or destroy a relationship.

3. Ask your parents to brainstorm solutions with you. Get a large piece of paper or poster board, and write your solutions to the problem on one side, and their solutions on another. See if you can come up with a matching solution. If your solutions don't match, try reaching a compromise in a calm way.

4. Comparisons are also hurtful and are not helpful. For example, "Carly's mom always lets her go to the mall without friends. She's such a better mom." Comparisons won't help you get your point across and they certainly won't help you get what you want.

5. Use "I" statements and avoid "You" statements. For example, "I felt embarrassed and hurt when you yelled at me in front of my friends. The next time you're upset with me, would you please pull me aside and talk with me instead of correcting me in front of my friends?" This allows your parents to know you are taking responsibility for your feelings while also being mature enough to offer solutions to the problem.

6. The most important part of communicating with your parents is that you do it daily. Too many times, we talk with our friends, but we forget about our parents. Why is THAT a problem? Because our friends don't have the power to make decisions for our lives, but parents do. Be smart and talk to the ones who can help make your life easier! Talk about everyday stuff with them and find out what's going on in their lives every time they ask about yours. If they

...our friends don't have the power to make decisions for our lives, but parents do.

don't ask about yours, ask them anyway. They will know you care, and don't just come to them when you need something.

7. Writing down what you would like to say can also be helpful if you find that you are nervous about talking with your parents. If your thoughts are organized ahead of time, you may feel more comfortable expressing your feelings and offering solutions to the problem.

So, what if your parents won't talk or listen to you? I know one teen girl who wants desperately to communicate with her dad, but he seems to have no time for her. She tells him she's on the honor roll and he mumbles, "That's nice" while reading the paper. She gets an outstanding grade on a project, but he says nothing when she shows him the project. Unfortunately, there are parents who are "checked out" or are too involved in their own world to meet us in ours. They make it difficult to talk with them and show little interest in what's happening in our life. When this happens, follow the steps we discussed earlier in this chapter. Confronting your parent in love to let them know you're not feeling heard can be a very powerful moment. If they keep ignoring you, find a trusted adult and share your concerns as well as your accomplishments with them. Success always feels better when we can share it with those who care about us.

If your parent continues to ignore you, be respectfully persistent in letting your parents know how important it is that you are heard. Tell them why it is important. Your dialogue may look like the following:

"Hi Dad." *(Dad grunts.)*

"May I schedule some time with you?" *(This raises Dad's curiosity a bit. He peers over the newspaper.)*

"Why?" Dad asks.

"I would like to spend some quality time with you when there are no interruptions. What would be the best time to do that this week?" *(You haven't asked Dad 'if' there is a good time, but "when.")*

"I'm busy this week," Dad snaps.

"Okay, I understand Dad. What would be the best time next week?" *(He realizes you are being politely persistent.)*

"I am really busy!" snaps Dad. "What do you want?" *(Dad is getting irritated now. Be respectfully persistent.)*

"I want to spend some time with you because you are my Dad and that's what Dads and kids do." *(True and heartfelt.)*

Dad sighs, "Okay. I guess next Thursday, but I only have a couple of minutes."

"Great! What time?" *(You're still not going away until he agrees to nail down a time.)*

"Four o'clock," Dad says as he dives back into his paper.

"Okay, where will we meet?" *(A respectful reminder that you're not going away.)*

"I don't know! Wherever..." *(Dad focuses all his attention back on the newspaper.)*

"Okay, then I'll pick. How about the park across the street?"

"Fine," grunts Dad.

"Thanks, Dad. See you then!"

You may only have a few minutes with Dad at that point, so make them count. If there is something you want to share, follow the suggestions listed in the previous pages. Time is precious and unfortunately, there are some parents who don't realize how quickly it slips away. While it hurts that our parents may not give us the time we want, we learn to use the time we have with them so that they hear our needs.

There may also be those of us who have the opposite situation. When parents demand our time or refuse to respect boundaries, we must still communicate respectfully. For example, what if you want to be a photographer, but your mom demands that you be a doctor?

When parents seem overbearing, one of the first things we have to do is try to find out *why* they are that way. For example, maybe your mom has dreams of you being a doctor because she wants you to be able to provide for yourself in ways she never could. Explain to your mom that you understand her concerns and allow her to express those. Listen calmly, and respectfully consider what she's saying. Next, express appreciation for her wanting you to succeed, and tell her how you plan to do that as a photographer. You may agree to disagree, but parents are often more understanding when they find out that you have a plan in place to succeed in life.

If you find yourself afraid to talk to your parents about certain topics, know that you are not alone. Approaching parents about embarrassing or uncomfortable topics can be hard. You may find the following lines helpful to begin a conversation with parents when you have to talk about difficult or uncomfortable subjects:

* "Mom, I need to talk to you about something, but it's kind of embarrassing."

* "Dad, I need to talk to you about something, but I'm afraid you're going to be mad and that I will disappoint you."

* "Mom, this is really uncomfortable for me to talk about, so thanks for listening."

* "Dad, I need your advice about something. Can we talk?"

You may also find yourself in moments when you don't want your parent's advice, you just need for them to listen. Try saying something like, "Mom, there's a problem that's really bothering me and I want to tell you, but I'm not ready for you to give any advice yet. Would you mind just listening?" This lets your parent know that you respect and need them, but that you would like some time to process your problem before they try to solve it for you. If your parent gives advice anyway, respectfully remind them that you asked them to wait and approach them about this issue at a later time. If it is a topic that you feel you need to share right away, find a trust-worthy adult and share with them. Sometimes, we just need to share things, and finding a trust-worthy adult who will listen is important.

There may also be times that you talk with your parents and they "freak out" or give a very strong reaction to whatever you tell them. For example, you like a guy that they don't approve of, and your parents make their disapproval more than known. They yell, say words that aren't in the Bible, and grab your cell phone so you can't talk to him.

When this happens, the best thing to do is to stay calm. While you may not like the WAY they are saying things, see if there is any value to WHAT they're saying. For example, "We don't want you to date that guy because he is on drugs." If that's true, then they have a valid reason to be concerned and you need to reconsider your choices because you deserve a better relationship.

If it's a false accusation, and the guy you like is not on drugs, listen for any other concerns they may have. Ask them why they believe he's on drugs, and take it from there. The key is to remain calm as you make your point known. The more you yell, argue or become defensive, the more you lose the chance that they will hear what you have to say.

Teens often tell me that one of the most frustrating areas they face is parents accusing them of getting an attitude when they are not. Parents often interpret silence as attitude because it's new for them. If we have yelled or argued in the past, parents may interpret silence as being belligerent. It is in your best interest to quickly let them know your silence is not intended to be disrespectful. It is intended to help you keep your emotions from taking over and saying something you will regret. Continue to show your parents that you're in control of your emotions. Hopefully they will soon understand that part of taking control of your life is learning to respectfully address your parents. A word of caution: if your silence IS being used as a tool to punish or control your parents, they will quickly recognize that and it WILL cause problems. Own up to your inappropriate use of silence and use it only in ways that work best for your relationship. Don't give your parents reason to say

> **Continue to show your parents that you're in control of your emotions.**

you have an attitude – you want to respectfully be in control.

Another frustrating area is when parents won't believe us. As teens, we want our parents to believe the best in us, but for whatever reason, they sometimes have a hard time trusting us. Maybe we have lied to them before, so they struggle to believe us or they gave us a second chance and we blew that one too. Whatever the reason, we have to do things that will help keep our parents' trust so that our life is easier.

How can we gain our parents' trust, even after we've lost it? Here are a few things to keep in mind:

* Keep your word. No matter how hard it may be or how unimportant it may seem, do it.

* Let parents know that they can trust you to be honest about who you're with, what's going on, where you are and what time you will be home. This will teach them that they can trust you with freedom.

* If your parents need to know something, let them hear it from YOU, first. Parents talk and you would rather your parents hear things from you than from your friend's parents.

* No sneaking out. Parents care about you and they want to know that you are safe at all times. Sneaking out destroys trust and causes you to lose the freedom you so desperately want!

* If you don't gain your parents' trust right away, keep doing the right thing. Eventually, they will see that they can trust you.

It is also important that YOU can trust your parents. Sometimes that's hard when you trust them with a "secret" and they tell others. When that happens, be sure to let your parent(s) know that you tell them things because you trust them not to tell others. Respectfully remind your parents that when they share your "secrets" with others it is hurtful and that you feel the same way they do when you break their trust. Assure your parents that you want to have a relationship with them that is filled with trust and give your parents another chance to keep your confidence.

If you find that you are unable to calmly communicate with your parents after putting all these suggestions into place, consider talking with a school counselor, youth director, pastor, or other trustworthy adult about your concerns. Be sure the adult you choose is someone your parents know and approve of, or someone you know you could introduce your parents to if they asked to meet them.

Communication is key to staying in control of your life and moving closer to the freedom you want. I will leave you with one of my favorite quotes:

"If you want your parents to improve, let them overhear the nice things you say about them."

—Unknown

Reflection:

> ➤ What do you find most challenging about talking with your parents?

> ➤ What can YOU do to help improve communication with your parents?

> ➤ What can your parents do to help improve communication with you? Are you willing to share this with them?

> ➤ What is one subject that is the most difficult to discuss with your parents? Is there anything different you could do that would make it easier?

> ➤ What is the most frustrating thing about talking with your parents? What can you do to help in that situation?

> ➤ What would your parents say is the most frustrating thing about talking with you? How can they help in that situation?

> ➤ What do you believe is the main reason teens don't talk with their parents? If you could give parents advice to help them understand why teens don't talk with them, what would it be?

CHAPTER SEVEN

The Tougher Questions

"Be strong when you are weak, brave when you are scared, and humble when you are victorious."

—*Unknown*

Sometimes, we find ourselves in teenage bodies facing what many would consider adult decisions. We may have created the situation we're facing or we may have fallen victim to someone's poor choices. Either way, we need answers.

The following are some tough questions that teens have asked me over the years and some of the answers I have given them. If you find yourself in any of these situations, I encourage you and your parents to seek counseling from your pastor or a trusted professional.

Q: How do I tell my parents I'm pregnant?

A: I pray that none of you reading this book will ever need this answer because this is a very scary place to be and one that no teen wants to face alone. No matter how close you are to your parents, not knowing how they or others will react is frightening. Planning the conversation is the first thing you will need to do. First, tell your parents, "I have something difficult to tell you. I'm pregnant." Don't say anything else. Allow your parents to absorb what you've just said. Then listen to what your parents have to say without interruption. While you have had time to process this news, they have not. Next, share your fears and worries with your parents. Let them know you do not take this lightly and that you know you are now responsible for another life. Finally, talk with your parents to decide if you will keep the baby or give the baby up for adoption.

Allow me to speak heart to heart with you. Some may tell you that abortion is also an option. While abortion is a short-term answer of convenience for you, your boyfriend, or family, it is murder. Abortion literally takes the life of another human being and dumps it like trash. You and your child are worth more than that, and your child deserves to live, even if it's with another family. Abortion may keep you from short-term embarrassment, but it's a decision that will haunt you for years and usually requires counseling to deal with the painful emotional aftermath. While family members may encourage you to "save yourself the embarrassment," I want to encourage you to "save yourself the lifelong heartache." When we make mistakes, people are much more likely to forgive us when they see us own up to our mistakes. You will never know if your baby was the one who would be President or cure cancer, and you can never know if they're not here. Do the most selfless thing you can do in this situation – let your baby live.

Q: I have written over 25 suicide notes. I don't really want to end my life, I just want someone to listen to what I'm going through, who will try to understand. Please help... I'm desperate.

A: First of all, suicide is NEVER the answer. Suicide lies to you and makes you believe that it will solve your problems when in fact, it is the enemy that steals EVERYTHING from you. Suicide wants to keep you from ever knowing what real love feels like, what real friends look like, and what feeling hope can bring. Suicide lies to you and says it's the permanent fix to your permanent problems. I have lived long enough to tell you that there is NO problem that will last forever. Tomorrow WILL be better. Tomorrow WILL bring new hope. It may not look the way you want it to look, but with the right people guiding you in your life as you make the right decisions, your life WILL get better.

Do not let suicide win. Talk to your parents about how you are feeling. If they are not helpful, go to your youth director, pastor, school counselor or other trusted counselor. KEEP GOING TO OTHERS until you find someone who will listen and help you get the support you need. Those who will sincerely help you will not judge you. After all, thoughts of suicide are not a "moral infraction," they are a desperate cry for help for something that is hurting on the inside. There are many who understand and are waiting to help you. There is also help available 24 hours a day on the "National Suicide Prevention Lifeline" by calling 1-800-273-8255. You will talk with trained, caring, supportive counselors who are there because they care about your life. We at Shannon Perry Ministries care about you, too! We love you and know that God has amazing plans for your life. Do not believe the lie that suicide tells you. There is help available when you reach out.

Q: My boyfriend and I have been dating for six months and I really care about him. Last weekend, he raped me. I have cried every day, feeling guilty that it was somehow my fault. I told him to stop, but he kept telling me it was okay and overpowered me. I just froze! Afterward, he told me not to tell anyone because they would look down on me and believe it was my fault anyway. How do I handle this? I feel so alone, hurt and afraid.

A: **The most important thing you must KNOW is that the victim of rape is *never* to blame.** If sex is forced against someone's will, it is rape. You never "owe" someone sex, no matter what they may tell you. Forced sex is an act of aggression and violence and one you can never "make" happen. The aggressor in the relationship has no respect for you or your values. He is selfish and usually lies to get what he wants. You deserve more. As hard as it may be, I encourage you to put your feelings aside about your attacker and end the relationship immediately. About half of those who are raped know their aggressor (New) so this can make dealing with rape even more complicated because there are feelings involved. Inspect the relationship and your feelings by answering the following questions:

1. Do I feel guilty for the rape that took place? If so, how did I "force" that person to rape me?

    A: You didn't because you can't force anyone to do anything. You're not that powerful.

2. Do I feel like I owe the person who raped me?

    A: You owe them nothing except possibly pressing charges against your abuser. His selfishness and control were what drove him to rape.

3. What do I do if I try to walk away and he continues to call because he knows I care about him?

    A: You put yourself out of his reach and realize that you deserve more. Do not answer his calls and if he continues to contact you in any way, notify your parents, record his phone calls, and report his actions to his parents and/or police.

The most important thing you must DO is to notify your parents and health officials *immediately* after the rape occurs, whether it is by a boyfriend, family member or a stranger. While this will be difficult, it is crucial for protecting yourself from future encounters.

Talking with a trustworthy adult who continually reminds you that the rape is not your fault is healing. Trying to overcome this on your own is a pitfall and does not work. Your experience does not make you broken, less than or used. It makes you a survivor.

Q: My Mom and Dad do not get along. They fight constantly, and sometimes I can't even sleep at night due to their yelling. It makes me so sad and I feel really alone because my other friends don't seem to have this problem. Please help.

A: It's really hard when people in our family are fighting. Feelings of anger, sadness and hurt are common when we are around a lot of fighting, especially when those arguing are people that we love. The first thing you can do is to talk with your parents. Let them know that their behavior is affecting your ability to sleep when they scream at night. Remind them that sleep is needed for you to do your best in school and that you know they want the best for you. Let them know how their fighting makes you feel and remind them that if they must argue, to please do so when you are not around and cannot hear them. After all, you are not responsible for your parent's problems, so you have no control over them. Family meetings are also a good idea. While it can be scary for kids to confront their parents, ask your brothers and sisters to join you in sharing how their fighting affects them. As a family, design a plan that is helpful to avoid fighting in the future. Outside counseling may be necessary for this plan to succeed, but your family and your peace of mind are worth it.

Q: I live with a family member who was diagnosed with an illness. I love them, but their illness takes up a lot of my time and energy. Some days are very demanding and I am feeling resentful that I have to live with this situation. I appreciate any advice you can offer.

A: First of all, you are not alone in feeling this way. Feelings of anger, stress, and even jealousy are common when someone's illness takes up a part of life that rightfully belongs to you. The most important thing to do in this situation is to take care of you. Talk with your parent or another trusted adult who can listen objectively to what you're feeling. Depending on the illness, you may want to join a support group with others who are experiencing illness in their own family. Talk with your school counselor if you are unsure how to find a group that is right for you. In the group, you will find comfort in realizing that others are experiencing many of the same things. You may also want to begin journaling. Getting your feelings down on paper helps identify many of the things that you are going through and can be very healing. Sharing your journal with a trusted adult like parents, your school counselor or youth director is also a great way to process many of the feelings you're experiencing. You may also want to find some things you enjoy outside of the house. Getting away from the environment occasionally helps keep balance in your life and keeps you focused on things you enjoy.

Q: I currently live with a foster family because my real mom is bipolar and unable to take care of me. While I really appreciate the love my foster family gives me, my heart is broken that I do not live with my "real" family. I feel guilty for feeling this way, and I'm angry that my "real" mom will not be a "real" mom to me. I feel rejected, alone and abandoned. How will I ever feel like I fit in anywhere?

A: I would like to answer this note on a more personal level. I had the honor of working with foster kids and their families when I was a school counselor. Those kids were some of the strongest, most appreciative kids I have ever met. They wanted to be loved and were so grateful for the help given to them by their foster families, but wanting their "real" parents to love them was always their desire. Your feelings about wanting your "real" mom are quite normal. My own son was not able to live with his "real" mom, but I can tell you, there's not a day that goes by that we don't know how blessed we are to have one another. I love him with all of my heart, and he loves me. I am not his "real" mom, but you would never know it by our relationship. I share that with you to give you hope. Right now, things may not be where you want them to be, but there is hope that you will find the love and acceptance you so desperately want, just as my son did when he and I found one another.

As you live with your foster family, here are a few things to keep in mind:

* It is not your fault that your mom is ill and there is nothing you could have done to help her. You are the child, no matter how old you are, and she is the adult. She needs adult help.

* Allow other adults who are trustworthy to help take care of you. Talk with a trained professional who is familiar with the anger, disappointment, fear, sadness and other feelings that go along with not being able to live with your "real" family. Sometimes when you share with others, you may feel a sense of guilt afterward as if you have said too much or become too vulnerable. That is a normal feeling, but you have not hurt anyone by opening up. You are learning how to become your best ally.

* Keep in close contact with your case worker. Your case worker should always have your best interest at heart. If you have problems in your foster family, your case worker is the one who needs to know. If there is ever abuse, neglect, or you feel uncomfortable in any way, you must talk it over with your case worker and allow

him/her to make decisions in your best interest. While this can also be frightening, you deserve the best care possible.

*   School counselors often work closely with case workers and they can become a great help to you. Talk with them regularly and discuss all the things you are feeling and experiencing in foster care. Remember... you are not alone and you did nothing wrong. There IS hope for you to be loved, nurtured, and cared for, and these steps can help put you on that path.

Appendices

APPENDIX A

Additional Scriptures

The Bible has a lot to say about the topics we have been discussing. I pray that the following scriptures are helpful as you study this book or when you need them throughout life.

Boys/Godly Husband:
Do not be yoked together with unbelievers. For what do righteousness and wickedness have in common? Or what fellowship can light have with darkness? What harmony is there between Christ and Belial? Or what does a believer have in common with an unbeliever?
2 Corinthians 6:14-15

Love must be sincere. Hate what is evil; cling to what is good. Be devoted to one another in love. Honor one another above yourselves. *Romans 12:9-10*

That is why a man leaves his father and mother and is united to his wife, and they become one flesh.
Genesis 2:24

Husbands, love your wives, just as Christ loved the church and gave himself up for her to make her holy, cleansing her by the washing with water through the word, and to present her to himself as a radiant church, without stain or wrinkle or any other blemish, but holy and blameless. In this same way, husbands ought to love their wives as their own bodies. He who loves his wife loves himself. *Ephesians 5:25-28*

Husbands, in the same way be considerate as you live with your wives, and treat them with respect as the weaker partner and as heirs with you of the gracious gift of life, so that nothing will hinder your prayers. *1 Peter 3:7*

Purity:
Above all else, guard your heart, for everything you do flows from it. *Proverbs 4:23*

Therefore, I urge you, brothers and sisters, in view of God's mercy, to offer your bodies as a living sacrifice, holy and pleasing to God—this is your true and proper worship. Do not conform to the pattern of this world, but be transformed by the renewing of your mind. Then you will be able to test and approve what God's will is – his good, pleasing and perfect will. *Romans 12:1-2*

Create in me a pure heart, O God, and renew a steadfast spirit within me. *Psalm 51:10*

It is God's will that you should be sanctified: that you should avoid sexual immorality; that each of you should learn to control your own body in a way that is holy and honorable. *1 Thessalonians 4:3-4*

Friendship:
My command is this: Love each other as I have loved you. Greater love has no one than this: to lay down one's life for one's friends. You are my friends if you do what I command. *John 15:12-14*

The righteous choose their friends carefully, but the way of the wicked leads them astray. *Proverbs 12:26*

Walk with the wise and become wise, for a companion of fools suffers harm. *Proverbs 13:20*

Do not be misled: "Bad company corrupts good character." *1 Corinthians 15:33*

Be devoted to one another in love. Honor one another above yourselves. *Romans 12:10*

A friend loves at all times, and a brother is born for a time of adversity. *Proverbs 17:17*

God Esteem/How He Sees Us:
Therefore, if anyone is in Christ, the new creation has come: The old has gone, the new is here!
2 Corinthians 5:17

Now if we are children, then we are heirs – heirs of God and co-heirs with Christ, if indeed we share in his sufferings in order that we may also share in his glory.
Romans 8:17

You are altogether beautiful, my darling; there is no flaw in you. *Song of Songs 4:7*

I praise you because I am fearfully and wonderfully made; your works are wonderful, I know that full well. My frame was not hidden from you when I was made in the secret place, when I was woven together in the depths of the earth. *Psalm 139:14-15*

She is more precious than rubies; nothing you desire can compare with her. *Proverbs 3:15*

Bullying/Kindness:
Do to others as you would have them do to you.
Luke 6:31

Do not let any unwholesome talk come out of your mouths, but only what is helpful for building others up according to their needs, that it may benefit those who listen. *Ephesians 4:29*

By this everyone will know that you are my disciples, if you love one another. *John 13:35*

Be kind and compassionate to one another, forgiving each other, just as in Christ God forgave you.
Ephesians 4:32

We who are strong ought to bear with the failings of the weak and not to please ourselves. Each of us should please our neighbors for their good, to build them up. *Romans 15:1-2*

Communication/Honor One Another:

Listen to advice and accept discipline, and at the end you will be counted among the wise. *Proverbs 19:20*

Honor your father and your mother, so that you may live long in the land the Lord your God is giving you. *Exodus 20:12*

Children, obey your parents in the Lord, for this is right. "Honor your father and mother" – which is the first commandment with a promise – "so that it may go well with you and that you may enjoy long life on the earth." *Ephesians 6:1-3*

The mouths of the righteous utter wisdom, and their tongues speak what is just. *Psalm 37:30*

Anxiety weighs down the heart, but a kind word cheers it up. *Proverbs 12:25*

Whatever you have learned or received or heard from me, or seen in me – put it into practice. And the God of peace will be with you. *Philippians 4:9*

APPENDIX B

References

"11 Facts About Human Trafficking." *DoSomething.org*. 25 Feb 2014. Web. 7 July 2015.
<https://www.dosomething.org/facts/11-facts-about-human-trafficking>

"Cyber Bullying Statistics 2014." *NoBullying.com*. 27 May 2015. Web. 7 July 2015. <http://nobullying.com/cyber-bullying-statistics-2014/>

Lyness, D'Arcy. "How Can I Help a Friend Who Cuts?" *KidsHealth.org*. Jun 2012. Web. 7 July 2015.
<http://kidshealth.org/teen/your_mind/friends/friend_cuts.html#>

New, Michelle. "Date Rape" *KidsHealth.org*. Oct 2014. Web. 7 July 2015. <
http://kidshealth.org/teen/your_mind/problems/date_rape.html#>

"Teen Pregnancy Facts." *TeenPregnancyStatistics.org*. Web. 7 July 2015. <
http://www.teenpregnancystatistics.org/content/teen-pregnancy-facts.html>

About the Author

Shannon Perry is an author, conference speaker, recording artist and TV host. Shannon holds a Master's Degree in Education and Counseling and is a Certified Instructor in Parenting Classes and Crisis Counseling. Shannon worked in the public school system for over fourteen years as a school teacher and counselor before entering full-time ministry. Shannon helped create an Anti-bullying program which is still used by one of the largest school systems in America. Shannon has one son who is a Captain in the U.S. Air Force.

Shannon is the creator of the "In Her Shoes" conference written especially for Moms and their teen daughters.

For more information or to join Shannon for an "In Her Shoes" Mother/Teen Daughter conference near you, visit ShannonPerry.com.

shannon_perry_ministries

facebook.com/shannonperryministries

More Inspirational Resources from Shannon

Available BOOKS

"The Overlooked Generation: Parenting Teens and Tweens in a Complicated Culture" covers topics such as dating, bullying, body image, social media, drug abuse, suicide and other important issues to help parents combat the onslaught of distractions that young people face today.

"Grace in High Heels" is a short chapter book filled with Shannon's hilarious stories. Each chapter contains scripture, a powerful life-lesson and discussion questions. Perfect for use as a devotional tool or book study.

Available MUSIC CD's

"Heirlooms" is a compilation of Shannon's favorite Christmas songs and hymns recorded after many requests over the years from family, friends and fans.

"The Real Thing" includes songs written especially for each topic of ***If the Shoe Fits***. Co-written with LifeWay writer/producer Paul Marino. Songs like *"Bad Hair Day"* and *"Keep On Pressing On"* garnered nationwide attention on radio. The song *"Long Way Home"* was written especially for Shannon's son Sean who serves in the United States Air Force.

Shannon's third CD, **"Tell the Story"** includes incredible music played by Grammy award winning musicians as well as songs that hit the national radio charts. Songs include *"Who's Gonna Love Me, God Is Doing Great Things, Tell the Story,"* and a song that Shannon sings especially for her dad entitled *"Love Never Ends."*

"Safe Place" is Shannon's sophomore project and includes seven original songs penned by Shannon including, *"David's Song,"* written for her husband, and *"Safe Place,"* one of the most requested songs that Shannon sings.

"Reflections," Shannon's freshman project, is a great variety of Southern Gospel and Light Contemporary. Songs like, *"Keep Walking On"* and *"Holy Ground"* are sure to lift your heart as you listen. Shannon sings, *"Thanks Again"* in honor of her mom and dad.

Available in AUDIO CD and DVD format
from the teaching series ***If the Shoe Fits***

"Goody Two Shoes" emphasizes the importance of balance and knowing our purpose. Jesus never had a Franklin Planner or a Blackberry, yet He lived the most balanced life of any man who ever walked the face of the earth. Through humor and scripture, Shannon reminds us that we will live balanced lives when we know our purpose.

In **"Lacing Up the Tongue,"** Shannon uses the practical illustration of a bridle along with scripture to remind us how we can heal or hurt those that we love the most by the words we speak. This session looks at the different tongues we want to avoid if we are to tame our tongue for God's glory.

Shannon shows us what scripture teaches about the promise of God's healing when we have been hurt in **"Is There a Hole in Your Sole."** Find out how to move forward into the amazing plans God has for us when we allow Him to have full control of the circumstances that hold us captive.

Holiness—we hear it often in church, but what does Holiness look like in today's world? In the session **"Walk A Mile In My Shoes,"** Shannon reminds us that there are practical ways that we can live Holy lives, and reminds us of the blessings we will incur when we "walk a mile in HIS shoes."

To order these available resources,
visit the online store at www.ShannonPerry.com.

You may also order at Chae Music via
Phone: 281-304-1278

Email: sales@shannonperry.com

Write: Chae Music,
P.O. Box 2887
Cypress, TX 77410-2887

shannon_perry_ministries
facebook.com/shannonperryministries

STAND

Notes

Notes

Notes

Notes

Notes

Notes

Notes

Notes

Notes

Notes

Notes

Notes

Notes

Notes

Notes

We want to hear from you! Please visit
Amazon.com and other on-line retailers to
write a customer review about

Stand